SO-ARE-508

THE GREEK TRAGEDY
IN NEW TRANSLATIONS

GENERAL EDITORS   William Arrowsmith
and   Herbert Golder

EURIPIDES: The Children of Herakles

EURIPIDES

The Children of Herakles

Translated by
HENRY TAYLOR
and
ROBERT A. BROOKS

OXFORD UNIVERSITY PRESS
New York   Oxford

OXFORD UNIVERSITY PRESS

Oxford   New York   Toronto
Delhi   Bombay   Calcutta   Madras   Karachi
Petaling Jaya   Singapore   Hong Kong   Tokyo
Nairobi   Dar es Salaam   Cape Town
Melbourne   Auckland

and associated companies in
Berlin   Ibadan

COPYRIGHT © 1981 BY HENRY TAYLOR AND
THE ESTATE OF ROBERT A. BROOKS

First published in 1981 by Oxford University Press, Inc.,
200 Madison Avenue, New York, New York 10016
First issued as an Oxford University Press paperback, 1992

Oxford is a registered trademark of Oxford University Press

All rights reserved. No part of this publication may be reproduced,
stored in a retrieval system, or transmitted, in any form or by any means,
electronic, mechanical, photocopying, recording, or otherwise,
without the prior permission of Oxford University Press, Inc.

Grateful acknowledgement is made to the editors of *Window* and *Dryad*,
for their hospitality to, respectively, lines 492–656, and lines 815–896.

Library of Congress Cataloging in Publication Data
Euripides.
The children of Herakles.
(Greek tragedy in new translations)
ISBN 0-19-502914-3   AACR2
ISBN 0-19-507288-X (pbk.)
I. Taylor, Henry, 1942–   . II. Brooks, Robert A.
III. Title. IV. Series.
PA3975.H6   1981   882'.01   81-2315

2 4 6 8 10 9 7 5 3 1
Printed in the United States of America

EDITOR'S FOREWORD

The Greek Tragedy in New Translations is based on the conviction that poets like Aeschylus, Sophocles, and Euripides can only be properly rendered by translators who are themselves poets. Scholars may, it is true, produce useful and perceptive versions. But our most urgent present need is for a re-creation of these plays—as though they had been written, freshly and greatly, by masters fully at home in the English of our own times. Unless the translator is a poet, his original is likely to reach us in crippled form: deprived of the power and pertinence it must have if it is to speak to us of what is permanent in the Greek. But poetry is not enough; the translator must obviously know what he is doing, or he is bound to do it badly. Clearly, few contemporary poets possess enough Greek to undertake the complex and formidable task of transplanting a Greek play without also "colonializing" it or stripping it of its deep cultural difference, its remoteness from us. And that means depriving the play of that crucial otherness of Greek experience—a quality no less valuable to us than its closeness. Collaboration between scholar and poet is therefore the essential operating principle of the series. In fortunate cases scholar and poet co-exist; elsewhere we have teamed able poets and scholars in an effort to supply, through affinity and intimate collaboration, the necessary combination of skills.

An effort has been made to provide the general reader or student with first-rate critical introductions, clear expositions of translators' principles, commentary on difficult passages, ample stage directions, and glossaries of mythical and geographical terms encountered in the plays. Our purpose throughout has been to make the reading of the plays as vivid as possible. But our poets have constantly tried to remember that they were translating plays—plays meant to be produced, in language that actors could speak, naturally and with dignity. The poetry aims at being *dramatic* poetry and realizing itself in words and actions that are both speakable and playable.

Finally, the reader should perhaps be aware that no pains have been spared in order that the "minor" plays should be translated as carefully and brilliantly as the acknowledged masterpieces. For the Greek Tragedy in New Translations aims to be, in the fullest sense, *new*. If we need vigorous new poetic versions, we also need to see the plays with fresh eyes, to reassess the plays *for ourselves*, in terms of our own needs. This means translations that liberate us from the canons of an earlier age because the translators have recognized, and discovered, in often neglected works, the perceptions and wisdom that make these works ours and necessary to us.

A NOTE ON THE SERIES FORMAT

If only for the illusion of coherence, a series of thirty-three Greek plays requires a consistent format. Different translators, each with his individual voice, cannot possibly develop the sense of a single coherent style for each of the three tragedians; nor even the illusion that, despite their differences, the tragedians share a common set of conventions and a generic, or period, style. But they can at least share a common approach to orthography and a common vocabulary of conventions.

1. *Spelling of Greek names*

Adherence to the old convention whereby Greek names were first Latinized before being housed in English is gradually disappearing. We are now clearly moving away from Latinization and toward precise transliteration. The break with tradition may be regrettable, but there is much to be said for hearing and seeing Greek names as though they were both Greek *and* new, instead of Roman or neoclassical importations. We cannot of course see them as wholly new. For better or worse certain names and myths are too deeply rooted in our literature and thought to be dislodged. To speak of "Helene" and "Hekabe" would be no less pedantic and absurd than to write "Aischylos" or "Platon" or "Thoukydides." There are of course borderline cases. "Jocasta" (as opposed to "Iokaste") is not a major mythical figure in her own right; her familiarity in her Latin form is a function of the fame of Sophocles' play as the tragedy *par excel-*

lence. And as tourists we go to Delphi, not Delphoi. The precisely transliterated form may be pedantically "right," but the pedantry goes against the grain of cultural habit and actual usage.

As a general rule, we have therefore adopted a "mixed" orthography according to the principles suggested above. When a name has been firmly housed in English (admittedly the question of domestication is often moot), the traditional spelling has been kept. Otherwise names have been transliterated. Throughout the series the -os termination of masculine names has been adopted, and Greek diphthongs (as in Iphigeneia) have normally been retained. We cannot expect complete agreement from readers (or from translators, for that matter) about borderline cases. But we want at least to make the operative principle clear: to walk a narrow line between orthographical extremes in the hope of keeping what should not, if possible, be lost; and refreshing, in however tenuous a way, the specific sound and name-boundedness of Greek experience.

2. Stage directions

The ancient manuscripts of the Greek plays do not supply stage directions (though the ancient commentators often provide information relevant to staging, delivery, "blocking," etc.). Hence stage directions must be inferred from words and situations and our knowledge of Greek theatrical conventions. At best this is a ticklish and uncertain procedure. But it is surely preferable that good stage directions should be provided by the translator than that the reader should be left to his own devices in visualizing action, gesture, and spectacle. Obviously the directions supplied should be both spare and defensible. Ancient tragedy was austere and "distanced" by means of masks, which means that the reader must not expect the detailed intimacy ("He shrugs and turns wearily away," "She speaks with deliberate slowness, as though to emphasize the point," etc.) which characterizes stage directions in modern naturalistic drama. Because Greek drama is highly rhetorical and stylized, the translator knows that his words must do the real work of inflection and nuance. Therefore every effort has been made to supply the visual and tonal sense required by a given scene and the reader's (or actor's) putative unfamiliarity with the ancient conventions.

3. Numbering of lines

For the convenience of the reader who may wish to check the English against the Greek text or vice versa, the lines have been numbered according to both the Greek text and the translation. The lines of the English translation have been numbered in multiples of ten, and these numbers have been set in the right-hand margin. The (inclusive) Greek numeration will be found bracketed at the top of the page. The reader will doubtless note that in many plays the English lines outnumber the Greek, but he should not therefore conclude that the translator has been unduly prolix. In most cases the reason is simply that the translator has adopted the free-flowing norms of modern Anglo-American prosody, with its brief, breath- and emphasis-determined lines, and its habit of indicating cadence and caesuras by line length and setting rather than by conventional punctuation. Other translators have preferred four-beat or five-beat lines, and in these cases Greek and English numerations will tend to converge.

4. Notes and Glossary

In addition to the Introduction, each play has been supplemented by Notes (identified by the line numbers of the translation) and a Glossary. The Notes are meant to supply information which the translators deem important to the interpretation of a passage; they also afford the translator an opportunity to justify what he has done. The Glossary is intended to spare the reader the trouble of going elsewhere to look up mythical or geographical terms. The entries are not meant to be comprehensive; when a fuller explanation is needed, it will be found in the Notes.

ABOUT THE TRANSLATION

The late Robert Angus Brooks was born of American parents in Calcutta in 1920. Educated in Scotland, he was graduated *summa cum laude* from Harvard, where he also took his doctorate in 1949. In 1942 he was elected to Harvard's Society of Fellows, before serving in the U.S.A.A.F.; after the war, he returned to Harvard as Instructor in Classics. A scholar in whom intellectual versatility and creativity were combined with administrative ability, he was at once—successively, but also consistently, throughout his life—teacher, poet, scholar, executive, public servant, and patriot. While teaching Classics at Harvard, he became involved with The Poets' Theater, in which he characteristically participated as actor, administrator and director (also of the Harvard production of *Oedipus at Kolonos*). The same versatility and scope were evident in his writing, which ranged from original poetry (published in *The New Yorker, Atlantic,* etc.) to a critical study of Frazer, to verse translations of Persius'

satires, and a book, Ennius and Roman Tragedy (New York, 1981).
For many years he was associated as executive and consultant with
Harbridge House, Inc. From 1965 to 1969 he served as Assistant Sec-
retary of the Army for Installations and Logistics. In the last years
of his life, from 1971 until his death in 1976, he was Undersecretary
of the Smithsonian Institution; it was during this period that he col-
laborated with Henry Taylor on this version of Euripides' Children
of Herakles.

Taylor, proclaimed by May Sarton as "the best poet of his generation," has published four books of poetry and is now working on
a long narrative poem. His first volume, The Horse Show at Mid-
night (1966), was followed by Breakings (1971). These were in turn
followed by An Afternoon of Pocket Billiards (1975) and Desperado
(1979). His poetry and critical prose have appeared regularly in most
of the country's better literary journals; he himself has given frequent
readings and lectures at many universities. In 1978 he received a fel-
lowship in creative writing from the National Endowment for the
Arts; in 1980 the Endowment for the Humanities awarded him a re-
search grant for a study of cultural stability in the agrarian community of Loudoun Valley, Virginia, where he was born in 1942.
After holding appointments in creative writing at Roanoke College
and the University of Utah, he settled in Virginia and accepted a
post as Professor of Literature at The American University in Washington, D.C.

As Brooks observes in his Introduction, Euripides' Children of
Herakles is an extraordinary play undeservedly neglected or, worse,
subjected to dismissive misreading. Yet the very features which
make it so interesting—its violently abrupt shifts of pace and tone,
its pervasive irony and odd blending of disparate modes—are themselves in large measure responsible for the play's neglect. They also
make the play unusually difficult to translate. And the lack of accurate and playable versions has meant that it is rarely read nowadays
except by professional students of Greek tragedy.

A remarkable play. Its rapidity of pace and tonal diversity are ex-
ceptional even for Euripides. And it abounds in those painterly
tableaux vivants (the arming of old Iolaos, the yoking of Eurystheus)
for which Euripides was famous. The resonance of epic is also everywhere audible, in the material and the language, but above all in
the (Homeric) values invoked explicitly and implicitly. But because
the poet has as usual anachronized his material into fifth-century

terms, this resonance is heard as a persistent thematic dissonance, which is in turn confirmed by the play's unconventional structure, its savage tonal shifts, and violent transitions. At first or second reading the varied episodes crowd past with what looks like wanton disregard for unity and thematic coherence. But then the pattern begins to emerge. Here and elsewhere Euripides is "the great master of peripeteia"; and the thematic counterpart of the play's jagged structure and choppy movement is that reversal of condition and fortune at which the finale so obviously aims. The same purposiveness is true of the tone, in which violent jostling of opposed modes—heroic and realistic, noble and vulgar, eloquent and colloquial, tragic and farcical, side by side, flatly confronting each other—makes the poet's strategy unmistakably plain. Here, as in *Hecuba*, *Herakles*, and *Andromache*, the dissonance is functional, pointed.

Take, for instance, the rejuvenation of Iolaos at the critical mid-point. The poet is manifestly striving to create the maximum possible incongruity, forcing the audience to assess what it has seen of Iolaos against the rejuvenation that the Messenger later reports. The miraculous transformation follows emphatically hard on the heels of the almost farcical scene in which we see the doddering old soldier armed for battle. Why, the reader asks, has the poet made the contrast so glaring? In part, as Brooks suggests, because the rejuvenation recalls a world in which divine and human purposes still converged; a time when Herakles' *arete* was rewarded with divinity and, in the person of Hebe, given eternal youth. But this mythical world is effectively undercut by the anti-heroic scene of Iolaos' arming. The armor which Iolaos dons is a venerable but antiquated relic of the glorious victory at Marathon when a handful of free Greeks—the *Marathonomachoi*—bravely stood off the slavish battalions of Persia. But those days are gone, gone forever. The effect, it seems to me, is bittersweet: a memory of lost innocence and archaic *arete* surviving into a more sophisticated and less noble age where, in Thucydides' words, "the ancient simplicity into which honor so largely entered was laughed down and disappeared." To this crossed perspective Euripides adds the pathos of old age, with its humiliating gulf between high aspiration and the body's incapacity to sustain the demands of the spirit which "ensouls" it. Finally, there is the dramatist's contextual emphasis: Iolaos' rejuvenation is reported briefly and matter-of-factly to an incredulous Alkmene. There is simply nothing here of the great religious diapason—elemental storm, divine and human purposes converging—that closes Sophocles'

Oedipus at Kolonos. Euripides' "theodicy" is ironically oblique, muted: a glancing image of what, in a world of nobler man and gods worthy of a noble man's worship, *might* have been the reward of human courage.

As so often, Euripides presents his theme in terms of polarities and contrasting orders. Against "things as they ought to be" is set the world of "things as they are"; against *logos*, *ergon*; against the fabulous and mythical, the gritty order of contemporary actuality; against the divinely aspiring spirit, the limitations of the mortal body. The purpose of this contrasting is not to expose one order in the name of the other, but rather, by means of their collision and dissonance, to describe the actual texture and tension of human life in a radically disjointed age. Thus the archaic *arete* of Herakles, incarnate in the nobility of Makaria, Iolaos, and Demophon, survives into the present where it confronts the moral baseness of late fifth-century political life (the choral "accommodation" at the close; Alkmene's brutality; the revelation of Eurystheus' epic *hybris* as nothing more than the fear-born policies of an ordinary man). Just as in Iolaos' case, where the body and spirit seem to part company, the body no longer able to "enact" the soul, so human society is divided into those who live and die nobly, and those who do not. At a still deeper level lies the ineradicable strain in human nature itself, perceived as an unstable mixture compounded of god and animal, always tense and at odds with itself. In their ensemble, what these polarities reveal is the dense ambiguity of the moral atmosphere, above all in the late fifth century, when the old existential tension of being human was violently exacerbated by tensions in the society and the culture generally. In such a world heroism may consist, as in this play and in Euripides generally, in the struggle to stay human.

This, I hasten to add, is my view of the play; in important respects it differs from that advanced by the translators in their Introduction. But one of the outstanding virtues of this new version is that it licenses the possibility of divergent interpretation. It is honest, accurate, conscientiously loyal to the Greek. Nothing has been skewed or warped in order to score interpretive points. The translators have their own forcefully argued view of the play's meaning, but they have carefully refrained from imposing their view upon the reader. In dealing with a play as elusive and ironic as *The Children of Herakles*, this seems to me the course of wisdom. A more conventional or arrogant translator would almost certainly have smoothed over the prevalent dissonance in order to produce a smoother and more acceptable texture. But this would mean stressing one polarity at the expense of the other; opting for the colloquial rather than the aulic or noble, or, conversely, exalting the heroic at the expense of the anti-heroic and pathetic. Either way the crucial tension disappears; the finely structured dissonance, the ironic balance, all dissolve. Iolaos must be *both* noble *and* pathetic. Makaria must not talk like a piece of virginal marble, "too good to be true"; her proper language is that of Euripides' self-sacrificing young people—Polyxena, Menoikeus, Iphigeneia—who speak, however naively, the language of absolute commitment. In Eurystheus' final speech, we should feel, as I think we do here, the simple unassuming candor of a man at last free—freed by death—to be himself.

If *The Children of Herakles* is not one of the greatest of Euripidean works it is nonetheless, as this version demonstrates, an extraordinarily rich play that deserves to be rescued from the Limbo of neglect. It deserves to be read. Read, and then reinstated. Ironically bleak and jarringly "offbeat" it may well be, but it is also a curiously moving and stageworthy play in which, once we adjust to the unorthodox structure and texture, the nature of Euripides' dramatic vision becomes unusually transparent.

Baltimore and New York   William Arrowsmith

CONTENTS

THE CHILDREN OF HERAKLES

INTRODUCTION

I

The *Herakleidai*, or the *Children of Herakles*, is an extraordinary play. It is even more extraordinary if we conceive it, as Greek plays too rarely are, in terms of action in the theater before an audience. It is at once rapid, fabulous, noble, and common to the point of comedy. It pursues concepts of deep moral grandeur and perplexity in the environment and often the language of the marketplace, the barracks, and the courts. It ends with a denouement of astonishing physical and ethical brutality. It may not be wholly successful. One could say the same about *Troilus and Cressida* or Ionesco's *Amedée*. But like them, it is remarkably alive because the playwright is pushing brusquely and with passion at the boundaries of his art.

II

The plot of the play is part of the complex of legends dealing with Herakles and his descendants. The legends, and the tangled dynastic relationships they involved, would be familiar to the audiences of Euripides' time, and the particular incidents depicted in the *Children of Herakles* would strike them with an overwhelming ironic force.

Herakles was the greatest and most universal hero of Greek legend. He was not constrained, like most of the other heroic figures, by time and place, but ranged over the entire Mediterranean world from the far west of Spain and Morocco (and perhaps beyond) to the fleshpots of Asia, encountering Titans from the pre-heroic world

3

and begetting sons to fight in the Trojan War at the end of the heroic cycle. His exploits drew upon his superhuman strength, often for the benefit of lesser men endangered by the savagery or obstacles of man and nature.

For all his strength, Herakles was cursed from his birth with misfortune and subjection to other men. He was the son of Alkmene by Zeus, and since his mother was of the royal house of Argos and Mykenai, he was the expected heir to the throne. Hera however, with her usual jealousy of Zeus' liaisons, managed to delay the birth of Herakles and hasten that of Eurystheus, his cousin, so that instead of becoming king, Herakles became Eurystheus' subject. To enforce this subjection and keep the hero afield, Eurystheus imposed on him the famous twelve labors. Herakles in fact was one of the few Greek heroes whose legend did not include a triumphant homecoming to his native land. For Oedipus, Theseus, Perseus, Odysseus, even Agamemnon, the return home was the summit of their story, even though terrible events might follow. For Herakles "home," in the person of Hera (patron goddess of Argos) and Eurystheus, her human agent, was his bitter enemy, never overcome, manipulating him like a slave in distant lands.

Herakles died in agony upon a pyre in Trachis, and according to the received legend was translated to become one of the gods. His tale of banishment and frustrated homecoming continued in a different mode with his children. Eurystheus sought to kill them, and they went into exile accompanied by their cousin Iolaos. Eurystheus continued to hunt them down, forcing each place where they took refuge to drive them out again, until at last they came to Attika.

Here Euripides' play begins. It was one of the boasts of Athenians that their city had given refuge to the children of Herakles, had settled them around Marathon, and with the help of Iolaos and Hyllos, Herakles' oldest son, had defeated Eurystheus' army and killed the king himself. The role of Athens as protector was a familiar one in legend. Oedipus (Sophocles' *Oedipus at Kolonos*) and Medea (Euripides' *Medea*) found refuge there, and Herakles himself was received earlier by Theseus (Euripides' *Herakles*). It was an easy theme for self-congratulation if Euripides had chosen so to use it.

The continuation of the Heraklid legend, however, had a bitter meaning for the Athenians. After Eurystheus' death, which closes Euripides' play, the children of Herakles and their descendants continued their effort to return home. Following a first abortive campaign to the Isthmus of Korinth which cost Hyllos his life, their descendants in the third generation marched south at the head of a Dorian army and overcame most of the Peloponnese including Argos, Mykenai, Sparta, and Messene. Their legendary conquest reflects the fact of the destruction of Mykenaian civilization in the twelfth century B.C. and the subsequent mastery of southern Greece by Dorian Greek tribes. Herakles' "homecoming," so long delayed, was accomplished at last in a tidal wave of violence and destruction.

Most of the nobility of the Peloponnese in historic times regarded themselves as descended from Herakles. In particular the Spartan kings traced their ancestry to two of the Heraklid conquerors of the Peloponnese. At the probable time of the play's production, one of the kings was preparing to march on Athens at the head of a Spartan army.

III

The *Children of Herakles* is not datable from external evidence, nor do we know the other plays which Euripides produced with it. Most commentators assign it to the early years of the Peloponnesian war, between 430 and 425 B.C. This is a reasonable dating on all known grounds. Unquestionably it is a play about war, and the effects of war within the state. In incidents and theme, it works upon the background provided by the great struggle between the Athenian and the Spartan alliances which began in 431 B.C.

Between them the two alliances controlled most of the Greek world except for Italy and the West. Thucydides tells us that "the growth of the power of Athens, and the alarm which this inspired in Sparta, made war inevitable." Inevitable or not, it was an appalling disaster. The war was to go on for a generation and end with the enfeebling of Greece, the defeat of the Athenian democracy, and the discrediting of its ideal of the free citizen. No one foresaw the catastrophe at first, but neither did any one doubt the significance of the conflict. There was patriotic exhortation on both sides, and mutual accusations of past sacrilege involving the murder of suppliants under religious protection. Once the war began, there was an almost hysterical reaction to the slightest reverses, particularly on the Athenian side. Perikles' strategy was to retain command of the sea, withdraw his land forces behind the walls of Athens, and let the superior Peloponnesian armies move virtually unchecked through Attika. This they did five summers in a row, ravaging farms and villages and probably by 427 sacking Marathon, the symbol of Athenian military heroism against the Persians and the location of Euripides' play. The outrage of the citizens, cooped up in Athens and helplessly watching their possessions being destroyed, put Perikles' leadership in jeopardy and led to his being fined by the Athenians before his death in 429.

The tensions of the war led also to a series of small but vicious atrocities, increasing with the progress of hostilities. A band of Thebans who had broken into the town of Plataia, an Athenian ally, early in 431 in the first act of hostilities, were killed by the Plataians after surrendering with a promise of safe-conduct. In 430 the Athenians captured by treachery Peloponnesian ambassadors to the king of Thrace, brought them to Athens, and murdered them without trial, although by custom the persons and ambassadors and heralds were sacred. They alleged retaliation for the murder of Athenian traders caught in the Peloponnese at the outset of the war. In 427 the Athenians voted to kill the entire adult male population of Mytilene in Lesbos and enslave the women and children for having revolted against them. Fortunately they had second thoughts the next day and stayed the order, killing "only" about a thousand of the leaders. Meanwhile the Spartans, taking Plataia after a two-year siege, killed all the surrendered Plataians who had been promised "the form of law" and destroyed the town. The events of this year culminated in the savage civil war at Kerkyra which Thucydides vividly summarizes:

Death . . . raged in every shape, and, as usually happens at such times, there was no length to which violence did not go; sons were killed by their fathers, and suppliants were dragged from the altar or slain upon it; while some were even walled up in the temple of Dionysos and died there. (III, 81)

It is not necessary to read specific topical reference to such events into the *Children of Herakles*. It is essential to understand that both Euripides and his audience were involved in them, whether in battles and killings or in the debates and decrees on military expeditions, judgment of leaders, and punishment of rebels. The climate of Athens in the years when the play was produced was an increasingly volatile mixture of bravado, sophistry, rage, and horror at the progess of a vicious conflict. Thucydides, writing later, saw at this point the crumbling of an essential element in Greek life: the relations between man and man, class and class, city and city.

The ancient simplicity into which honor so largely entered was laughed down and disappeared; and society became divided into camps in which no man trusted his fellow. (III, 83)

A sense of this decay, and of what was being destroyed, is at the core of Euripides' intention in the *Children of Herakles*.

IV

The first impression of the play in action is one of compression and breakneck speed of development. It is one of the shortest plays in the existing Greek repertoire, running for about an hour and fifteen minutes, but it contains enough incident for two or three plays of normal length.

Iolaos appears first with the young sons of Herakles at the altar before the temple of Zeus at Marathon. He explains his position as companion and kinsman of Herakles, and after his death, as guardian of his children with Alkmene, Herakles' mother, who is inside the temple with her granddaughters. He tells of their pursuit by Eurystheus, and has barely finished when Eurystheus' herald bursts upon the stage. Kopreus is the spokesman and agent of force.[1] After a brief angry exchange with Iolaos, he lays hands on the children and attempts to drag them from the altar. Iolaos intervenes and is knocked down. Another hasty entrance follows: the Chorus of citizens of Marathon. They prevent the herald's design and interrogate Iolaos, who enters his group's claim to sanctuary as suppliants. Kopreus argues with the Chorus but breaks off at the entrance of the king of Athens, Demophon, son of Theseus. All this has taken about seven or eight minutes on stage.

The rapid development continues in argument. The herald and Iolaos present their cases to Demophon, who decides for the suppliants. Kopreus, undaunted, offers the king a slippery excuse for giving them up to him, fails, and tries again to seize one of the boys. Demophon is prevented from striking him down only by the Chorus, and Kopreus goes off threatening Argive retaliation. After a short ode, Iolaos and the children offer formal thanks to Demophon and the Chorus. Demophon leaves to prepare the city for war. Iolaos remains at the altar to pray for victory.

Up to now the plot of the play has been the formal equivalent of the whole *Suppliants* of Aeschylus, which tells a similar story with

---

1. His name is not given in the play. It means "dung man." He was traditionally the herald of Eurystheus.

parallel incident. It is condensed to one-third the length of Aeschylus' play. Euripides rushes on. Demophon returns with an oracle requiring a virgin's sacrifice, which he refuses to impose on his city. Iolaos futilely offers himself to buy off Eurystheus. Makaria, Herakles' daughter, comes out from the temple and insists upon being the victim. She goes off with Demophon. A servant appears to announce to Iolaos and Alkmene the return of Hyllos, Herakles' oldest son, with an allied force to join the Athenians. Iolaos suddenly decides to enter the battle, obtains arms and struggles off with the servant. After another ode, a messenger runs on to report the battle, the bravery of Hyllos, the cowardice of Eurystheus, the victory of the Athenians and Heraklids, the miraculous rejuvenation of Iolaos, his pursuit and capture of Eurystheus, and the imminent arrival of Eurystheus as prisoner. In an extraordinarily complex and condensed final scene, Eurystheus is brought in; Alkmene vengefully demands his death and meets opposition from the Chorus and messenger who tell her that Athenian law requires prisoners taken alive to be spared. Eurystheus answers with fortitude, composure, and a prophetic vision that his grave will help Athens against the descendants of the Heraklids when they invade Attika. Alkmene browbeats the Chorus with this new argument for executing him. They agree. The play ends abruptly.

The movement of the play seems all the more brusque because no single character occupies a dominant role. The children of Herakles, who are the characters of the title, are on the stage and highly visible throughout, but do not say a word. They maintain an enigmatic silence at the center of the turbulent action. Among the other characters, Kopreus, Demophon, Makaria, Iolaos, and the messengers appear, disappear, and are not seen again. Alkmene enters the action late, and Eurystheus, the presumed villain, at the very end. Dramatic attention is continually being shifted from one character-grouping to another. None of the individual parts has time or mental room within the play to develop or to internalize the dramatic action.

External action is plentiful. The play is full of physical activity; the use of physical objects (wreaths knocked from the altar, Demophon's staff, Iolaos' armor) and physical contact between the characters (Iolaos and Kopreus, the servant and Iolaos, Alkmene and Eurystheus) tend to insist upon a realistic and almost a knockabout environment. The language matches this. Though recognizably the language of tragedy, it is plain and spare for the most part, and some of the most striking images are common, even crude. Kopreus compares the effect of war to stepping into the bilge of a ship. Demophon says (253)* that if he were to give up the suppliants to Argos it would be a "hanging crime." Other more traditional images are sometimes used ironically. When Iolaos in the prologue (13) says that he has Herakles' children "under the dwindling shadow of my wings," he is using a phrase from Aeschylus, where it signifies divine protection, but he obviously means to contrast the confidence of that image with his present feeble and powerless condition (14): "I defend them—though I need defenders of my own."

The institutional furniture of the play too is deliberately contemporary and everyday. The talk is of law-courts, legal claims, jurisdiction over runaways. Demophon is chosen king by lot like an Athenian archon; he marshals his army like an Athenian *strategos*; his soldiers are Athenian heavy infantry of the fifth century. The whole question of refugees and sanctuary on which the play turns is one of intense topical interest to the Athenians of the time.

The play presents itself initially then as a rapid, almost bewildering series of actions, played out in an environment immediately familiar in important ways to its audience—the rush of public business in a democratic state, and specifically in a democratic state at war for its life. Events are not generated by the participants; they press in upon them. Decisions must be made on the spot; once they are made new crises and alarms arise; public reaction is instantaneous and must be dealt with. The business is not ended even with a victory; there are the issues of the aftermath. Under the pressures of such a time, people do not behave with composure and gravity; they scuffle, they grab weapons, they collapse in despair.

The familiarity is intentional. Euripides of course was to write several plays with a comparable wealth of incident and activity, for instance the *Orestes* and the *Iphigeneia at Aulis*. He was to write others which deliberately emphasized a contemporary and everyday environment or characterization, like the *Elektra*. But in no other play did he combine and compress these two devices to such effect as in the *Children of Herakles*. His intent is to hold a mirror to the spectators, and in the absence of a commanding dramatic hero, to involve his audience in the significance of the play and in the deep questions which work through its troubled action. The play generates such questions, and thrusts them outward to the watching community.

* Unless otherwise indicated, line references throughout are to our English version.

V

It is fair to ask: are there in fact any deep questions or problems of the human condition developed in the *Children of Herakles*? Or is such a hurly-burly play merely intended as an exciting wartime diversion, catering to the natural desire for images of Athenian courage against the Peloponnesian enemy, Athenian nobility in protecting suppliants, and the pious assurance of ultimate divine favor and protection for Athens? The weight of critical opinion about the play is affirmative to this last question. Ours is opposed.[2]

Within the turbulent action of his play, Euripides sets himself at first to develop the theme of an ideal nobility of action which is accessible to the free citizen and brings him into harmony with the divine order. Moral complications are stripped away in order to clarify his proposition. The Chorus and Demophon are confronted with a ready-made act of violence, both civil and religious, on the part of the Argive herald, the attack on suppliants in a sacred precinct, so that their judgment is never in doubt. The herald's arguments for giving up the suppliants rest ultimately on force and nothing else, the superior power of Argos to enforce its decrees anywhere in the Greek world (272-73):

DEMOPHON This is my country. Here, I am king.

KOPREUS So long as you don't provoke the Argives.

His thesis would be familiar—and not merely as a denunciation of the attitude of Athens' current enemies. Thucydides was to put a similar sentiment into the mouths of the Athenian ambassadors to Sparta before the outbreak of the war, in defense of Athens' own imperial policy:

. . . it has always been the law that the weaker should be subject to the stronger. (I, 75)

In any case, the argument is uncomplicated, and the risk is vividly presented by Kopreus. It is nothing less than death, destruction, and the reduction of Athens to a subject status. The city can avoid the first two only by accepting the third. Demophon responds without hesitation; he will protect the Heraklids come what may.

2. It is not the function of this Introduction to engage in detailed critical polemics. We should like to cite two commentaries on the play which have provided especially sympathetic and useful insights: G. Zuntz, *The Political Plays of Euripides* (Manchester, 1955), and P. Burian, "Euripides' *Heraclidae*: An Interpretation," *Classical Quarterly*, LXXI (1976).

His reasons and the way in which he states them are vitally important. Greatest, he says, is Zeus, since the suppliants are at his altar and under his protection. Next is kinship between the Heraklids and himself, and his father Theseus' debt to Herakles. Finally, with a curious reversal of priority, he says (249-52):

Third, dishonor—which should be the first of my considerations.
If I allow strangers to desecrate this altar,
men would charge that Athens was no longer free,
that I had betrayed a suppliant out of fear of Argos.

The ambiguity is crucial to the theme of the play. Demophon and the other characters accept religious obligations (the protection of suppliants) and injunctions (the oracle) with conventional piety. They never question them, but do not feel them as a personal spur to action. The relationship of the action to the gods is largely placed in the mouths of the Chorus. The real motivation, Demophon says, for himself, is the sense of disgrace before the human community at large in showing fear and abandoning his city's freedom. Iolaos has already introduced this theme as a reason for his faithful guardianship of the children of Herakles after their father's death. If he failed them, he says, people would speak of him with contempt. Again, in countering the herald's arguments, Iolaos assures him that Athens will respect the same standard (208): "Brave men fear dishonor more than death."

Against the herald's arguments of power, therefore, both Demophon and Iolaos are appealing to that sense of restraint from viciousness and impulse to decency which has its roots in the opinions and expectations of the surrounding community, and which often goes under the untranslatable Greek term *aidōs*. Iolaos in fact uses the word almost at the beginning of the play, as furnishing the motivation for his whole career. The concept is older than Homer, and is often linked with an aristocratic outlook and ethos, but remained powerful among the Greeks of the fifth century. Perikles, in Thucydides' account, gave it a preeminent place in his funeral oration over the Athenian dead in the campaigns of 431 B.C.:

But all this ease in our private relations does not make us lawless as citizens. Against this, fear is our chief safeguard, teaching us to obey the magistrates and the laws, particularly such as regard the protection of the injured, whether they are actually on the statute book, or belong to that code, which, although unwritten, yet cannot be broken without acknowledged disgrace. (I, 38)

We need not assume that Athenians of the Periklean age always acted on the precepts of aidōs. But it remained important in men's minds and emotions, along with the complementary sense of confidence that their interests and standards were shared by others in the community. It was precisely this kind of unwritten standard of trust that Thucydides saw beginning to break down with the strains of war, to be replaced by the justification of deceit and atrocity. At this point in his play, Euripides is saying with Perikles that despite the pressures and within the democratic institutions of his city, there is still room for the "ancient simplicity."

Demophon's determination is soon overturned by the oracle which demands the sacrifice of a girl of noble family to Persephone. He accepts the oracle's injunction without question, as do all the characters in the play. But it leaves Demophon at a loss (429-31). There is no noble solution for him. In justice,

> I will not kill my own daughter,
> nor will I compel any Athenian to such an act
> against his will.

He appeals to the Heraklids for help. Iolaos again without hesitation offers himself, but the king declines with realism as well as courtesy. On cue, Makaria comes in. She is the most idealized picture of nobility in the play. As soon as she learns the situation, she demands to be sacrificed (518-19):

> I'll be your sacrifice. Unforced, of my own free will,
> I volunteer my life.

A few lines later, she firmly rejects Iolaos' proposal that the lot be used to choose among her and her sisters. In doing so, she recalls to us the similar choice made by Theseus, Demophon's father, who had volunteered among the young people normally chosen by lot to be sent to Crete and sacrificed to the Minotaur. By her action, Makaria too saves Athens, but there is no question that she does it as a Heraklid and to safeguard the seed of the house of Herakles. Almost her last words, spoken to her brothers around the altar, are (608-9):

> In the place of children
> I will never have, these are all my treasures . . .

The noble decision by Athens is not enough; it needs a reciprocal gesture from the strangers it protects to save both city and suppliants. In providing it, Makaria appeals to the same sense of aidōs and the opinion of men that motivates Demophon and Iolaos. Like Iolaos, she imagines vividly what others will say if she shirks her duty to die and wanders once more to seek refuge. Surely other cities would expel her for such cowardice. In her mind, outraged opinion would be even stronger than the religious injunction to protect the suppliant.

The whole character of her appearance makes her a kind of apparition. There is a curious anonymity throughout this scene. Makaria is not called by her name (it is known only from the list of characters and other sources of the legend), and after her exit disappears entirely from the play.[3] She comes, she acts, she does what is necessary for "my father's daughter," (546) and she departs.

One further action completes the theme of nobility; it is gratuitous and not prompted by outside events like those of Demophon and Makaria. In the next scene, Iolaos hears of the arrival of Hyllos with an army and questions the messenger with growing excitement. As the man breaks off to return to the battle lines, Iolaos cries out (706):

We think alike. I'm going with you. Friends help friends.

The play has emphasized Iolaos' old age and feebleness. He has spoken of it himself. The herald has thrown him to the ground, and he has just been seen collapsed and almost insensible with grief at the sacrifice of Makaria. He now proposes to go into battle from a simple sense of honor and duty, again motivated by a respect for the world's opinion (725-26):

Only a coward would stay here, safe behind walls,
while others do our fighting for us.

The effect is first one of pathos, like the picture of old Laertes preparing to fight with the suitors at the end of the Odyssey, or Priam at Troy, or the blind king of Bohemia at Crécy. But the ridiculous too is not far away, and Euripides stresses both to a point almost unparalleled in extant Greek tragedy. He has established the framework of common life earlier, and here the everyday world, in the person of the servant-messenger, answers by mocking the impulse of nobility which presents itself in such unlikely decrepitude (707-11).

SERVANT Sir, this is no time for foolishness.

IOLAOS Foolishness? To fight in my own cause?

3. Except for a brief reference to human sacrifice in the messenger's speech reporting the victory.

SERVANT Sir, you're not the man you used to be.
  IOLAOS I'm still man enough to handle a spear.
SERVANT Man enough—provided you don't stumble.

Up to this point we have been given images of nobility acting in harmony with democratic ideals and institutions (Demophon), then appearing from among the refugees in a savior role (Makaria). But Iolaos' extreme and quixotic intention seems too much. The play's environment and its theme are placed in confrontation. We are invited to laugh, but the laughter is almost painful. A few minutes later, Iolaos leaves on the servant's arm. He stops to appeal to his lost strength (766-69):

Oh, gods, give me back
the strength of this good right arm of mine!
Make me what I was when I was young
and at Herakles' side, I took the city of Sparta!

We realize that he too is perfectly aware of his weakness, but is still determined to take his place in the war.

    The denouement of this action is against all expectation. Another messenger returns to report to Alkmene the victory of Athens and the Heraklids. Nobility is justified, the suppliants are saved, and the words of the Chorus in the ode just before the battle link the human success to a divine endorsement. Then the messenger goes on to report a miraculous change in Iolaos. In Hyllos' chariot, he has pursued Eurystheus from the battlefield. In answer to his prayer for strength (880-87),

Suddenly, two stars, all blazing fire, settled down
    on the horses' yokes, hiding the chariot
    in a kind of cloud or shadow.
Men who understand these things said those stars
    were Hebe and your son, Herakles.
Then, out of that darkness in the air came Iolaos—
    young, his strong shoulders straining on the reins,
    a man in all the vigor and freshness of his youth.

Even if the change is only for one day, as Iolaos has asked, it goes far beyond any expected divine justification and enters the realm of fantasy. But it is a fantasy that transforms the perceptions of everyday life. Everything that Iolaos in seeming folly has said he will do, he has done; everything that the common-sense servant has ridiculed, that the Chorus have decried, that Alkmene has called madness, has come to pass. A key to Euripides' meaning is found in another play, the *Madness of Herakles*. There the Chorus, speaking of old age and youth, say:

If the gods were wise, and understood
what human wisdom understands
second youth would be their gift
to seal the goodness of a man. (655-59)[4]

In that play, the Chorus deny the possibility of such a gift. Here the gods have bestowed it. The earlier scenes show human characters pushing the values of "human wisdom" to their limit. Their choices are simply made, by the old standard of aidōs and from the impulse to satisfy the expectations of their community and mankind. They accept the framework of necessity established by events and the gods, and do not appeal to it for justification. There is no theodicy in their minds. But the choices they make are by no means easy, entailing the risk of destruction, self-sacrifice, and death in war. At this point, as if in recompense, the gods adopt human standards. They show that they understand "what human wisdom understands" and glorify the hero with the gift of youth, while justifying the other sacrifices with victory.

VI

The play seems complete. But there is one more turn, a short scene of a hundred-odd lines that totally reverses all that has gone before and closes the drama with brutal shock instead of heroic fulfillment.

Immediately after the news of Iolaos' rejuvenation, the messenger relates the epic capture of Eurystheus by the new hero, and his imminent arrival in chains as Iolaos' spoil of war. It is most probable that Euripides invented this incident. In the more usual version of the legend, Eurystheus died in the battle at the hands of Iolaos or Hyllos. Euripides' intention is soon clear. Eurystheus has been the most powerful king in Greece, but also the ultimate source of violence and evil throughout the play. The vicious herald Kopreus has been only Eurystheus' creature. Alkmene asks with some amazement why Iolaos spared his life. In the messenger's answer, Euripides begins to show his audience a more repulsive side of their popular ethos (913-18):

4. Translated by William Arrowsmith, to whom we are also indebted for suggesting this passage. Euripides used the theme of rejuvenation and a second life elsewhere, as in the *Suppliants* (1080-87). It must have played a major part in his lost play *Daughters of Pelias*, which was his first production in 455 B.C.

> He was thinking of you.
> He wanted you to see Eurystheus yourself—
> see him subject to *your* will, *your* slave.
> Eurystheus, of course, resisted—so they used
> force, they yoked him. He had no wish
> to meet your eyes and suffer your revenge.

This is audacious. Euripides is using one of the most popular and most obscene tricks of the stage: to build up fear and hatred of a powerful and evil character, then to show him helpless and humiliated to the audience and to invite them to gloat righteously over his physical torture and mental agony. There is more than a frisson of that suggested pleasure in the messenger's speech. When Eurystheus is dragged on in chains, Alkmene fulfills the expectation. She abuses Eurystheus verbally and physically (there is no question of this from her language), rehearses her old grievances against him, and finally pronounces his death sentence. In the fetid atmosphere of this set-piece of revenge, there is nothing so far unusual in this.

But both the servant in charge of Eurystheus and the Chorus intervene. She cannot kill him, they say; the Athenian rulers have decreed that Eurystheus, having been taken alive, must be kept alive. Hyllos has agreed. We are suddenly reminded of what the play has been about, the achievement in action of honor and just dealing among men, and we realize that Eurystheus and Alkmene have changed places in a particularly menacing way. She is now the agent of unbridled violence; he is the intended victim under the protection of the same Athenian state. But is the popular will still allied to lawful action and compassionate behavior? Certainly the Athenians who had seen the Spartan ambassadors dragged through the streets to the death-hole or perhaps had voted for total vengeance on the surrendered Mytileneans, might be of two minds.

Alkmene responds to this check with fury. She insists that she will kill Eurystheus with her own hands. She specifically and scornfully rejects the claim of community opinion and female *aidōs* (1006-8):

> Call me what you like, call me cruel,
> say I'm more arrogant than woman ought to be—
> but this man *must* die, and *I* will do it.

Here Eurystheus himself speaks for the first time, and produces yet another reversal within the play. He has been described as tyrannical and cowardly, owing all his success to good luck, but his speech is that of a brave man, facing death with indifferent calm. He will not beg for his life. He defends his behavior by casting the blame on Hera, but he recognizes that it was a sickness, and generously praises Herakles. He tells Alkmene that in his place, she would have acted exactly as he did, and we recognize a deadly truth in this. He asserts the religious nature of the decree which spared him, and the religious pollution that will fall upon his executioner. Eurystheus does not clear himself of his crimes, but his whole bearing is a moral confirmation of the decision to save his life. It is not merely now a question of keeping an enemy prisoner alive but also of killing a man of courage and sensibility.

But the Chorus, representatives of the Athenian will, have already begun to waver. They have told Alkmene that her anger is understandable. Now they "advise" her once more to let Eurystheus go (as though she were the ruler of Athens), but when she offers a way to satisfy both the law and her lust for killing Eurystheus, they grasp at it eagerly (1053): "That would be best." Her proposed solution turns out to be a horrid sophistry: she will kill him, then "obey the city" by delivering his body back to the Argives. In this she echoes Kopreus who has used a similar play on words in demanding that Demophon give up the suppliants. There Demophon angrily rejects the proposal. But here the Chorus say nothing in reply. From this point, there is no doubt of the complicity of the Chorus in Alkmene's actions.

Instead, Eurystheus speaks once more. In recompense for Athens' clemency (literally, a derivative of aidōs is the word he uses) he will present it with an ancient oracle: his own body buried at Pallene will be Athens' savior and the enemy of the Heraklids when they return as invaders (obviously referring to the current war with Sparta). In Eurystheus' words there is a translation from the human theme to that of the sacred hero, whose body and burial place retain an immortal power to influence human events. The hero is addressed by cult words supplied by Eurystheus himself: "avenger" and "noble." He places himself beyond the sphere of common mortality, like Oedipus, who was also buried in Attika at Kolonos. But Oedipus did not die by human hands. Within the framework of this play, the oracle offers to the Chorus and Athens a pragmatic and political excuse for closing their eyes to Eurystheus' murder. Alkmene seizes upon it and characteristically pushes it even further. "What are you waiting for?" she cries (1079); "Kill him. Now." She draws the Chorus into the act that she said earlier she would do herself, and in her rage disregards the fact that her own descendants will suffer from it. She even tells the guards to throw Eurystheus' body to the dogs, an injunction so shocking and so at variance with the prescription of the oracle that some editors have sought to emend the text. But to all this the Chorus merely reply in the last speech of the play (1087), "We agree," and go on to assert that the Athenian rulers are free of pollution. The play ends on this note of self-serving exoneration.

It is inconceivable that Euripides shared this view, that he wanted to present Alkmene as some evil and alien will, embodying perhaps the hated Spartans of the time, and the Chorus' action as merely prudent and reasonable in securing Athens' future. He has shown Alkmene along with the Heraklids taken under the protection of Athens and received into the Athenian community, in part through their own courage and self-sacrifice. Her participation is emphasized several times by Iolaos, and she is the only one of the group whose name Makaria actually uses with affection and reverence in her final speech. Whatever her significance, she is a member of the community.

Euripides has also taken care to present the episodes of Makaria and Eurystheus in parallel and contrast. In both, an oracle has defined the conditions of action, and in neither do any of the characters question the validity of this definition. But in the first case, one of the Heraklids themselves comes forth with the purest nobility to offer herself to death and thereby save Athens as well as the suppliants. In the second, another of Herakles' family, also a woman, comes forth with repulsive savagery to insist on murdering a man who is under Athens' protection. After the first act, the Chorus show a full if conventional appreciation of Makaria's sacrifice in almost Periklean terms (644-48):

Even as she dies, this girl discovers
    deathless honor and glory in giving up her life
    for her brothers, for all of us.

The glory she leaves behind her will shine forever,
    as noble actions outshine the darkest pain.

After the second, they can only say "we agree." Euripides leaves us with this appalling reversal of judgment, and of the communal ethos which underlies it. Cold-blooded advantage has triumphed, aidōs and the loving fantasy of harmony between gods and noble men which it has brought about have been blotted out. The play in its completeness creates and springs from an almost unbearable sense of loss, the wasting away of that "ancient simplicity" which was recognized by Thucydides too at the moment of its departure.

VII

In the final scene, the Chorus emerge as the central figures of the play, responsible for decisions that are crucial to the action and its meaning. If the *Children of Herakles* fails, it is in this respect. For Aeschylus, the Chorus could be full participants, even principal characters, in both external and internal action; he used them as such in his *Suppliants*, *Eumenides*, and *Agamemnon*. Both Sophocles and Euripides abandoned not only the dramatic device but the whole style and dramatic concept of which it is a part. Their Choruses occasionally take part in the external action as *ad hoc* partners or opponents of the principal characters,[5] but never in a decisive role and far more usually as lyric commentators upon the action. Euripides, even if he had wanted to, could not return to the Aeschylean model, and in this play he did not perfect a new technique answering to the role which he thrust upon the Chorus.

It is worthwhile to recapitulate the Chorus' function in the *Children of Herakles*. If there is a key to production of this tense and difficult play it is in the interpretation of the Chorus as a subliminal "role-player," and in the relations thus established with the central theme.

The Chorus first appear in swift, disciplined intervention in the action, just as Kopreus has thrown Iolaos to the ground and is attempting to lay hands on the children at the altar. One part of the group interposes between Kopreus and the children; the two leaders question Iolaos, ascertain his case, assert religious prohibition and their own civic freedom against Kopreus' violence, and announce the arrival of the Athenian kings. In the next scene, their leader again intervenes to prevent Demophon from committing a sacrilegious act by striking the herald. Immediately then the Chorus establish a participating role as civic representatives and active guardians of secular and religious standards in the state. As the play continues, they relinquish this direct intervention and develop their theme principally through a succession of choral odes. The first follows the expulsion of the herald and the adoption of the Heraklids into the Athenian community. It is a simple, almost balladlike de-

5. Such plays are the *Iphigeneia in Tauris* and the *Orestes* of Euripides, the *Oedipus at Kolonos* of Sophocles, and the *Rhesus*.

fiance of Kopreus, Eurystheus, and the Argives. It has been called "jingoistic," but it does not spring from mindless patriotism; it rests on an appeal to decent common opinion which is outraged by violence offered to suppliants in a free community. This is exactly the reason that Demophon has given earlier for his decision to protect the Heraklids. City and king are united in their stand, and the play emphasizes the voluntary and essential nature of this sympathy.

The second ode follows Makaria's departure. It has been called "flat" and "unoriginal." But again we have seen how the tone and even the language grow from the Chorus' civic role. It does not represent the lyric reflection of the poet, but rather the restrained and formalized expression of condolence and praise appropriate to the city's funeral oration over the heroic dead. It is clear that the Chorus are themselves being "characterized" in these odes as within the sphere of action, rather than "characterizing" the action from an outside point.

The third ode follows Iolaos' fantastic and seemingly foolish departure to the battle. The three odes therefore relate to and complement the three principal stages in the "noble action" of the play. The third takes a bold step beyond the others. It is a battle-ode like the first. The Chorus have already presented the arguments of common sense against Iolaos' resolve, but the first strophe of their ode strikes a new chord, more lyrical than anything that has gone before and more in tune with the old hero's fantastic enterprise. They call upon all nature—earth, moon, sunlight, to shout to heaven in an actual summons to the gods. "I"—the city, the Chorus—will now go into battle (779-81):

We're ready, ready to take up shining steel, ready to fight
for these guests of ours, for Athens,
    for glory, and home.

In the mouths of the Chorus, this is startling and essentially unparalleled in Greek tragedy. It implies direct participation in the battle, and it would not seem out of place to have some members of the Chorus arm and follow Iolaos off stage. At the same time, there is none of the sturdy defiance of the first ode here, or of the bravado that casually places Athens' strength equal with Argos'. Rather (782-84),

Oh, day of shame when Mykenai,
arrogant in her swelling power,
came breathing hatred against our city.

The rest of the ode grandly develops the theme that human justice and right action, placing themselves in such peril, demand the support of the gods (794-95):

> Our justice, our courage deserve
> their home, deserve to hold and keep this land forever.

The Chorus carry the justification of the actions of their city, and of the suppliants whom the city has taken in, beyond the realm of common opinion, to the level of divine order. They go into battle looking for a sign from the gods, as if they themselves were the protagonist within the drama.

In the next episode, they receive it, in the form of victory and the miracle of Iolaos' rejuvenation. The last choral ode follows, celebrating the victory and the revealed divinity of Herakles. It is an extraordinary composition. The first words (923):

Sweet, the dance is sweet

speak of the Chorus' own role (generically, not as a dramatic chorus) as a celebrating group of singer-dancers—but as it were from the outside, as though they were the citizens watching a performance. The following language and the whole structure of the ode suggest the performance of another form of lyric: the choral odes celebrating victories in the Olympian and other pan-Hellenic games. Pindar, the greatest lyricist in this form, had died about ten years before the play's production, but others were still composing. Euripides' ode here suggests the structure often used by these poets:

1. The comparison of glorious or beautiful things to the present occasion: "A is great (lovely), and B, but it is most joyful to celebrate this victory." Compare Pindar, *Olympians*, I and XI.
2. Praise of the victor and his qualities, in this case the city. The victory is related to divine favor.
3. A mythic reference, often critical of other versions, and appropriate to the victor—here the marriage of Herakles and Hebe.
4. A moral or gnomic sentiment closing the ode.

The Euripidean Chorus transforms itself for this occasion into a group performing a rite of celebration for victory which would suggest a noble, aristocratic, and faintly archaic character. On the stage, concerted with the music and movement of the dance, this could have a stunning theatrical effect. The democratic city and its representative Chorus, the same people who argue on street-corners, go to court or to battle, and bustle about the city's business, finally lay hold upon a world in which individual human excellence arising among them is paid supreme honor, and nobility consorts easily if transiently with divine favor.

It is from this world that the Chorus are wrenched into the horrors of the final scene. The last gnomic words of their ode are (951):

May such passionate ambition never be mine.

They are immediately confronted with the insatiable rage of Alkmene. They protest, waver, and collapse into acquiescence. It is perhaps too much, too rapid, too brutal for an "acceptable" dramatic framework. Perhaps this was Euripides' intent. The assumption of individual responsibility to the community which brings forth the purest heroism under the press of events in war can also incorporate the arbitrary will, the assumption of individual license which bring forth unbridled cruelty, vengeance, and self-interest. If the play ends with a hero in defeat and moral disintegration, that hero is the civil body of the city, and not only the Chorus as its representatives, but also the real community, strained to a danger point under siege, the spectators in the Theater of Dionysos.

VIII

It remains to provide some notes on characters and on the production of the play for an audience. We have dealt with the characters as they advance the themes of the play and have noted that in the compression of action and multiplicity of actors there is little room for depth of character explanation and development. There is no Medea, no Hippolytos, no Herakles here (though all these plays date from the same period of Euripides' dramaturgy). But neither are the characters mere busy and lifeless puppets. Euripides illuminates each one swiftly and surely, enriching dramatic function with personality. Even the messenger roles have this individuation. Alkmene's slave who brings the news of the victory is supple, quick, and flamboyant in his vivid descriptions. At the end of the scene, he takes a lewd enjoyment in Eurystheus' desperate struggle for death against his capture and bondage, only to become a slave in Alkmene's hands—then quickly and brashly reminds Alkmene that she has promised him his own freedom for the news. He is an able, outspoken soul, deeply poisoned by his servitude. The other messenger is Hyllos' servant who tells Iolaos of his master's arrival with an army. He is probably the same as the messenger in the last scene who brings on the captured Eurystheus. This is a wholly different personage, a bluff, loyal countryman, familiar and laconic in his description of war and princes, and nonplussed to the point of derision by Iolaos' sudden resolve to join him in the battle.

The young king, Demophon, not only is the perfect nobleman in his dissection of his royal responsibilities, but also shows the necessary touch of inexperience and uncertainty when confronted with the oracles. He wants very much to be a good king, to enjoy mutual dealing in justice with his people. But he sees no way to do it while obeying the oracles, and at last turns to old Iolaos with the confession (491): "I've seen the oracles; and they terrify me."

Even Makaria, that isolated figurine of nobility, makes a quick and intense impression of intellectuality as well as virtue. Every one of her speeches is a kind of public reasoning with herself, from her first entrance, stating and then rebutting her own reluctance to come out in public, through her rapid enumeration of all the unacceptable contingencies if she shirks her duty, and her instant rejection of the choice by lot proposed by Iolaos, to her last speculation on the possibility of an afterlife. Her presence conveys little pathos and much power; in her brief appearance she overshadows the other characters.

The most expanded character in the play, and the most fascinating, is Iolaos. He is the old nobleman, maintaining the same code as Demophon, but no longer having the power to enforce it. And yet he is very far from being simply a pathetic study in feeble old age. From his appearance at the beginning of the play, his words have an ironic bite and mastery in each situation (1-2):

For a long time now, I've lived by this law:
the good man is born to serve others.

It is the central theme of the play, but as Iolaos develops it here, we understand his implication: the good man does himself no good at all, in the vulgar sense of the word. He describes his guardianship of the children ironically with an Aeschylean phrase. He understands why other cities have driven them out (27-28): "they wilt/in the face of power." He is quick to grasp the implication in Demophon's appeal for help in the face of the oracle; it is that the Heraklids should voluntarily leave Athens once more, and spare the king the agony of choice. Iolaos creates an impression of self-knowledge and knowledge of others which inform his prickly sense of honor, his impetuousness, and his feeble physical strength. It is of course the

Greek kind of self-knowledge, not of psyche and motivation, but of one's position in the scale of powers, one's mortality, one's degree of subjection and that of others to the conditions of life, fate, and necessity, that is comprehended in the phrase gnōthi seauton, "know thyself." Iolaos' knowledge is unflinching, and it extends in time. He knows what it is to have been a hero, and he knows what he is today. It leads him to offer Herakles' children to Demophon even as slaves; it would be better than the obliteration of their race forever. From such a base his passion and fantasy spring up with increased power and credibility. When he speaks of praising Demophon to Theseus his dead father, and we realize that for all his ironies he accepts quite simply the underworld of the Homeric age, the dead heroes walking the fields of asphodel in converse with each other, the effect is moving. Again, he speaks with a terrible and human truth (623), after Makaria has gone out to her death with his praises in her ears:

This is a cruel deliverance.

And in his last scene, as he struggles with the armor and stumbles on his way to war, we cannot help but hope that somehow that piercing knowledge is still with him.

Alkmene has been Iolaos' partner and twin marshal in all their trials and wanderings. They are of the same age, at least for the purposes of the play.[6] Although she does not appear until late in the play, her name and the fact that she is nearby in the temple are kept constantly before the audience. When she comes forth, it is soon clear that she is Iolaos' opposite in every sense. She is a model of irredeemable ignorance—of self, of others, of the situation. She does not wait to be told who the messenger from Hyllos is, but is ready to fight him as a herald from Eurystheus. Her words are those of non-comprehension, and she soon retires from the animated dialogue between Iolaos and the messenger. So far she might seem good-hearted if dull-witted. But later in the scene when Iolaos leaves her finally to the protection of Zeus, she says with scorn (745-47),

Zeus?
Zeus will never hear a word of reproach from my lips,
but Zeus knows best how he's treated me.

6. Actually, in the usual version of the myth, Iolaos was the son of Iphikles, Herakles' mortal twin, and therefore the grandson of Alkmene, like the Heraklids. For Euripides' purposes this was impossible. He therefore avoids all mention of Iolaos' specific relation to Herakles' family and refers only to a general kinship. See the genealogy in the Note to 213.

Something perhaps may be permitted to one who has been Zeus' consort, but in the play this is a jarring and vulgar note. No other character speaks of the gods or their actions in this spiteful tone. In her ignorance of the human station, the menace of Alkmene begins to show. It bursts forth after the victory. She assumes that Iolaos' sparing of Eurystheus' life is a clever trick. This is the level of her understanding. It is never raised. Her lust for vengeance, when Eurystheus comes before her, reduces every inkling of thought to an animal cunning which serves her only goal. Her position as a suppliant taken into the community of Athens, the laws of the country, the opinion of man, even the safety of her own descendants, go by the board. Her stated sufferings simply do not justify it. She is the demon of self-ignorance and self-interest, raised up out of Euripides' dark apprehension of his time, and coming only too vividly true in reality as his play came to the stage.

The difficulties and possibilities of the Chorus as "character" have already been outlined. They are usually described as old men of Marathon. They are certainly at Marathon, the scene of the play, and Demophon addresses their leader as "old." Beyond this the Chorus are not characterized, nor do they, like many other Greek dramatic choruses, describe their own composition and status. Also, Euripides does not make much of the possible association with Marathon, still a rich symbol of heroism for the Athenians. After an initial fix on the location, the Chorus and characters refer to their city exclusively as Athens. It is most tempting, therefore, in the light of the different *personae* assumed by the Chorus in their odes to think of them as a diverse group representing the range of the Athenian citizen body—young and old, city men and country men, rich and poor, soldiers, assemblymen, traders. Such a composition would at once provide a comprehensive frame for the "noble action," not limited to a single class or place, and would help to explain the final helplessness of the Chorus in the face of Alkmene's demands.

A significant question of staging, finally, is the relationship of the silent children of Herakles to the other characters and to the developing action of the play. Their presence alone must create a certain tension; it would be impossible to forget that the descendants of these boys created the Spartan state and the Spartan kings. Their interaction with Iolaos, Kopreus, Demophon, and Makaria is fairly well suggested by the language of the play. But how do they react to Hyllos' messenger, to Alkmene, to Eurystheus, and finally to the

Chorus, especially in the last scene? Euripides left no stage directions here; but it is impossible to think that as the play's producer he neglected the silent force which these characters could give to his theme.

IX

We have based the translation upon the Budé text edited by Louis Méridier, as providing the best overall guide among the considerable textual difficulties of the play. Departures from that text are signaled in the Notes.

We are grateful to Donald C. Goertz, who assisted in the preparation of early drafts of the translation. The playwrights David Kranes and Thomas Phelps read an early draft, and made many valuable suggestions. The National Translation Center made a small but indispensable travel grant at a crucial stage of the composition. William Arrowsmith, the Herakles of his time, has expended enormous amounts of energy in advising and encouraging us; we are deeply grateful for his criticism, and for his example. Our wives, Frannie Taylor and Jane Brooks, have made many suggestions, typed many pages, endured many spirited readings of odes and speeches, and have in countless other ways earned more of our love and gratitude than we can express. We dedicate this book to them.

Washington, D.C.   ROBERT A. BROOKS
October 1975

Lincoln, Virginia   HENRY TAYLOR
July 1980

THE CHILDREN OF HERAKLES

CHARACTERS

IOLAOS guardian of the children of Herakles
SONS of Herakles, half a dozen boys, seven to sixteen years old
KOPREUS herald of Eurystheus
CHORUS of citizens of Marathon
LEADER of Chorus (a second chorister acts as "Second Leader" in one scene)
DEMOPHON king of Athens
AKAMAS brother to Demophon
MAKARIA daughter of Herakles
ALKMENE mother of Herakles
SERVANT of Hyllos, Herakles' son
MESSENGER slave of Alkmene
EURYSTHEUS king of Argos and Mykenai
GUARDS two spearmen who escort Eurystheus

Line numbers in the right-hand margin of the text refer to the English translation only, and the notes at p. 72 are keyed to these lines. The bracketed line numbers in the running headlines refer to the Greek text.

The scene is Marathon, near the eastern coast of Attika. The stage building represents the temple of Zeus; it has one entrance, in the center. Before the temple stands a simple altar: a waist-high rectangular block of stone, placed on a stone base a few inches thick and some eighteen inches longer and wider than the block itself. A few simple wreaths, made from leafy branches, have been placed on the altar.

As the play opens, IOLAOS, an old man, stands near the altar. The SONS of Herakles are grouped around the altar, sitting or kneeling on the base. IOLAOS addresses the audience.

IOLAOS For a long time now, I've lived by this law:
       the good man is born to serve others.
       The man who devotes himself to his own advantage
       is a dead weight in any common enterprise,
       a useless burden, good for nothing but himself.
       This, years of hard experience have taught me.
       I could have left the world alone,
       living a life of privacy and peace in Argos;
       but compassion—compassion, and the bond of blood—
       compelled me to become Herakles' only partner   10
       in his great labors, when he was still with us.
       Now that he's gone among the gods, he leaves
       his children under the dwindling shadow of my wings.
       I defend them—though I need defenders of my own.

       After Herakles had left this world,
       Eurystheus wanted us dead, so we ran away.
       We lost our country, but we saved our lives.
       Now we wander like fugitives, hounded

from town to town. Outrage after outrage:
after all our suffering, he still pursues us.   20
He discovers our whereabouts, and then immediately
dispatches a herald after us, demanding
we be surrendered, like runaway slaves.
So our would-be allies are forced to choose
friendship with us, or war with Argos. No choice there.
They look at us, a handful of wretched orphans
with an old feeble guardian, and they wilt
in the face of power, and drive us out.

Now I share exile with these children here—
exile, hopelessness. I can't betray them.   30
People would say, "You see,
now that their father is dead, look how quickly
Iolaos, their only kinsman, has deserted them."
Now we're outcasts, everywhere. So in the end
we came here, to Marathon, as suppliants
seeking asylum at this altar of their gods,
asking protection one last time. We know
that this country is now ruled by Theseus' two sons,
who inherited it when the descendants of Pandion
divided the kingdom. They are our cousins.   40
And so, our wandering has ended here
at the boundaries of Athens. Shining Athens.

Two old, unlikely marshals lead this march of ours
to nowhere. Myself, worn out from fending
for these boys; and Alkmene, their grandmother,
who's minding the girls inside the temple there.
It would be a shameful thing for young girls to stand here
outside, exposed to public crowds before this altar.
Hyllos and the older boys have gone ahead
to look for still another sanctuary.   50
Even here, we might be refused—
                              Quick, boys,
here! I see Eurystheus' herald, on his way
to make us fugitives again.

The SONS *assemble behind* IOLAOS *as* KOPREUS *enters.*

                              Gods,
how I detest you—you and your king!
When I think how many times you came to Herakles
mouthing your demands, threats—humiliation on
     humiliation—

KOPREUS So here you are. You think you're safe, do you?
You think the people of Athens will fight for you?
Madness.
                    No sane man would choose your helplessness
when he might choose the power of Eurystheus.   60
(*moving toward* IOLAOS) On your feet.
No more stalling. On your feet and come with me.
You'll get the justice you deserve in Argos—
death by stoning.

IOLAOS   Not to Argos.
This altar of the gods will protect me.
So will this earth on which we stand.
This earth is free.

KOPREUS Must I use force?

IOLAOS You won't take me or these boys. Not by force.

KOPREUS Then you're no prophet.   70

     Tries to seize one of the SONS; IOLAOS *struggles with him.*

IOLAOS Not while I'm alive.

KOPREUS Out of my way!
(*knocks* IOLAOS *down*) These boys are going back
to Eurystheus. Back where they belong.

IOLAOS Help! Men of Athens! Help! Look—suppliants
at Zeus' altar—forced away—our wreaths trampled—

an outrage to your city—sacrilege to your gods—

Enter, from right, CHORUS of citizens of Marathon. In dress, height, style, and age, they represent various types of citizenry. In this scene two men divide the LEADER's speeches.

LEADER What's going on here?

2ND LEADER Why this brawling at the high altar of Zeus?

LEADER Look, an old man, knocked down, lying here—
this is shameful . . .   80

2ND LEADER (*to* IOLAOS) Who did this?

IOLAOS (*indicating* KOPREUS) That man. He did it.
He dragged me from the altar, insulted your gods.

Members of the CHORUS confront KOPREUS, interposing between him and the suppliants. The two LEADERS continue to question IOLAOS.

LEADER You, sir—who are you? Where are you from?
How did you get to Marathon?

2ND LEADER Or did you come here by boat, from Euboia?

IOLAOS We're not island people, strangers.
We come from Mykenai.

LEADER Your name?

IOLAOS Iolaos. Squire and companion of Herakles.   90
You may have heard of me.

LEADER Yes, I remember hearing your name in the old days.
But who are these boys?

IOLAOS The sons of Herakles. We came here

(motions to SONS, *who kneel before* CHORUS*)*

as suppliants to you and your city.

LEADER   Why are you appealing to the people of Athens?
         What is your request?

IOLAOS   We want protection. We ask for sanctuary.
         We ask not to be returned by force to Argos.

KOPREUS   (*to* IOLAOS) I warn you: it won't sit well with your   100
              masters,
          if they find you here. They have power over you.
          Even in Athens.

LEADER   (*to* KOPREUS) Stranger, the rights of suppliants must be
             respected.
         There can be no violence at the altar of the gods.
         Here, justice rules. Violence is forbidden.

KOPREUS   Surrender these children to Eurystheus,
          then there'll be no question of violence.

LEADER   I tell you, it would be sacrilege
         to ignore a suppliant's appeal to our city.

KOPREUS   I warn you once more. You're risking trouble.   110
          In this case, prudence would be best.

LEADER   Practice your own prudence. My advice to you is this:
         explain to our king why you've acted
         as badly as you have here. Don't outrage
         our gods by tearing suppliants from sanctuary.

KOPREUS   Who's king here?

LEADER   Demophon, son of Theseus.

KOPREUS Then I'll take my case to him.
Talking to you is wasting words.

LEADER Here's King Demophon now—Demophon and his brother
Akamas.   120
They'll hear your charges.

Enter, from right, DEMOPHON *and* AKAMAS. *Both are young
men, simply dressed.* DEMOPHON *carries a staff.*

DEMOPHON (*to* LEADER) Old man, I commend your vigilance.
You were prompt—quicker than our young men, I see—
to answer a cry for help. Now,
why are these people kneeling here at the god's altar?

LEADER My lord, these are the sons of Herakles.
This is Iolaos, Herakles' friend and squire.

DEMOPHON But why all this brawling?

LEADER That stranger there, the herald, tried
to drag them from the altar. They shouted for help.   130
Then he knocked the old man down. It was pitiful.

DEMOPHON In dress, in style, this man looks Greek.
His behavior is barbarous.

(*to* KOPREUS) All right,
stranger, who are you? Where are you from?

KOPREUS Since you ask, I am Argive, from Mykenai.
King Eurystheus dispatched me here
with orders to return these fugitives to Argos.
I am provided, sir, with legal claims to present.
I have authority to act. I am here as an officer of Argos,
empowered to take formal custody of Argive runaways,   140
fugitives from Argive jurisdiction.
They have been condemned to death by Argive law.
As a sovereign state, Argos has the right

to execute the verdicts decreed by its own courts
against its own subjects. Again and again these runaways
have sought sanctuary at altars throughout Hellas,
but our position has been consistently the same,
and no Greek city has dared to risk the reprisals of Argos.
Either they thought that Athens was mad,
or they themselves were mad with desperation,   150
ready to stake all on this last appeal;
in any case, they have sought asylum here.
How, otherwise, could they have dreamt that Athens—
Athens alone, of all cities in Hellas—
could let compassion outweigh the claims of common
          sense?
Compare; then decide whether it's wiser
to harbor these fugitives, or surrender them to us.
This is what you gain from us: the power of Argos
will be yours; the great strength of Eurystheus, your ally.
But if you soften, swayed by their sorry tale,   160
hard steel will be our answer.
Don't suppose that Argos will concede without a fight.
And what pretext would Athens have for war?
That we had robbed you, annexed your land,
attacked your allies? And when you bury your dead,
for what great cause will you claim your soldiers fought
          and died?
Imagine the gratitude of your citizens,
if, for the sake of one doddering fool—
this walking charnel house, this ancient zero—
and this clutch of miserable brats,   170
you and your city founder in the bilge.
Your only argument is hope—a hope
worth far less than what lies in your hands.
Perhaps you like to think these boys will grow up
and fight for you. But even then,
they could never cope with the army of Argos. Meanwhile,
the Argives will have ample time to conquer you.
Believe me. Do as I suggest. Concede me nothing,
simply let me have what is mine by right,

and, by so doing, gain Mykenai's friendship.
Abandon your old way of siding with the oppressed.   180
Why choose weak friends when you could have strength?

LEADER No case can be judged, not
        until both sides are presented and debated.

IOLAOS Here, in this place, my lord, I have the right
        to speak, not only the right to listen.
        You will not drive me away, as others before you have,
        not until I present my case to you.
                I have no legal argument with this herald here.
        These children and I ceased to be Argives   190
        when our sentence was decreed, when we went into exile.
        So how can he claim that we are Mykenaians still?
        How can they banish us, then hunt us down?
        We are aliens, outcasts.
                            (to KOPREUS) Or is it your argument
        that exile from Argos means exile from Hellas?
        Surely Athens is open to us still.
        The men of Athens have no fear of Argos;
        they'll welcome, they'll protect the sons of Herakles.
        Athens isn't Trachis, or some small Achaian town.
        Athens is none of those places from which you've driven   200
            us before—
        driven us, not because you had a right, but because
        you flaunted your Argive strength, exactly as you're doing
            now.
        Everywhere you showed contempt for the rights of
            sanctuary
        afforded by the altars of the gods.
        If that can happen here, if Athens can be cowed by Argos,
        then Athens is not the city, the free city I have known.
        But I do know the Athenian spirit; they'd rather die
        than yield this point. Brave men fear dishonor more than
            death.
        I say no more. Excessive praise, I know, is tiresome.
        (to DEMOPHON) My lord, let me explain why, as leader of   210
            this country,

it is your duty to protect these boys.
First, they are your relatives by blood.
Pelops' son was Pittheus. And Pittheus had a daughter,
Aithra. She was the mother of Theseus, your father.
Now Herakles, the father of these boys, was the son
of Zeus by Alkmene, granddaughter of Pelops.
So, Demophon, your father and their father were cousins,
which means you're bound to them by blood.
But you have other obligations too.
Once, as Herakles' squire, I sailed with him and Theseus   220
to win the belt of the Amazon queen.
Many brave men died on that expedition. And all Hellas
knows how Herakles brought your father Theseus
home alive from the blind world below.
In return for Herakles' help then, his sons ask you now:
Do not surrender them. Don't let them be driven
from the altars of your gods, expelled from Athens.
You would be disgraced before all Athenians
if homeless suppliants, your own cousins—
look, look at these boys!—were haled away by force.   230
(*kneeling*) I beg you,
by your knees, your hands, your beard,
protect the sons of Herakles.
Adopt them as your own sons. My lord,
make yourself their friend. Be kind. Be their cousin.
Be their father, their brother. Be their master, even,
before you hand them over to the Argives.

LEADER   My lord, when I hear what these people have suffered,
I pity them. I have never seen nobility
so abused by fortune. What they suffer,   240
they should not suffer. It is wrong.

DEMOPHON   Iolaos, three considerations compel me
to honor your request.
                              The first argument
is Zeus, before whose altar you now kneel
with this holy gathering of god-protected children.
Second, old debts and ties of blood

demand that I protect them—
they are the sons of Herakles.
Third, dishonor—which should be the first of my
    considerations.
If I allow strangers to desecrate this altar,   250
men would charge that Athens was no longer free,
that I had betrayed a suppliant out of fear of Argos.
A disgrace, a hanging crime.
I wish you had come on some happier mission. . . .
But courage. Don't despair. *Here* you and these boys
will be safe from all violence, I promise you.
(*to* KOPREUS) As for you, stranger herald,
go back to Argos, give Eurystheus my answer.
Tell him, if he thinks he has a legal claim
against these people, our courts will give him fair hearing.   260
But I will *not* surrender them. Not to you. Never.

KOPREUS   Even if I prove my claim is just?

DEMOPHON   Just? How can force be just?
Or driving suppliants from an altar?

KOPREUS   The disgrace and risk are mine, not yours.

DEMOPHON   It would be disgrace to hand them over.

KOPREUS   Then banish them. I'll seize them at the frontier.

DEMOPHON   Fool, do you think you can outwit the gods?

KOPREUS   Criminals, it seems, find asylum in Athens.

DEMOPHON   All men find asylum at the altars of the gods.   270

KOPREUS   The Argives may disagree.

DEMOPHON   This is my country. Here, I am king.

KOPREUS   So long as you don't provoke the Argives.

DEMOPHON Better anger the Argives than the gods.

KOPREUS War with Argos, then? An ugly prospect.

DEMOPHON Agreed. But I will not abandon these suppliants.

KOPREUS So you say.
         But they're mine to take, and I'll take them.

DEMOPHON Then you'll find your homecoming hard.

KOPREUS (*attempting to seize a child*)

         Let me put your courage to the test.   280

DEMOPHON (*raising his staff to strike* KOPREUS)

         Touch them, and you'll regret it. Now—

LEADER In the name of god, don't strike a herald!

DEMOPHON I will if he forgets he's a herald.

LEADER Leave, stranger.
        My lord, his person is sacred.

KOPREUS (*moving away*) I'm leaving. I am not strong enough,
         or fool enough, to fight you all.
         (*from a safe distance*) But I'll be back, and with me
         an army of invincible Argive soldiers.
         Even now, at the frontiers of Megara, ten thousand men,   290
         under arms, Eurystheus at their head, are drawn up,
         waiting to learn the outcome of my mission here.
         When Eurystheus hears your insolent answer,
         a tide of iron will sweep over Attika,
         destroying everything you have—
         your people, your land, your crops, everything you have.
         If we failed to take revenge,
         all the martial vigor of Argos would flourish for nothing.

DEMOPHON Be damned to you! I'm not afraid of Argos.
You won't take these children. Or my honor either.   310
Athens is a free city, not a colony of Argos.

Exit KOPREUS, *followed by* AKAMAS. *As they leave, the*
CHORUS *turn to each other, speaking individually and*
excitedly.

CHORUS —Now is the time to make ready,
now, before the Argive army reaches our border.
—The war god of Argos is savage, brutal,
more brutal now than ever before.
—You know how heralds bluster, always the same.
—Their reports always magnify the facts.
                          —Twice as large!
—Imagine his lies.
                —Imagine what he'll tell his king.
—The outrage,
              —the insult to his person,
how he barely,
          —barely,
                —escaped
                    —with his life.   310

IOLAOS The best, the finest heritage a son can have
is a noble and courageous father.
In the hour of hardship, when ordinary men weaken and
      fail,
nobility stands firm. Look where we stood:
we thought we had no hope. And then
we found allies, found kinsmen here in Athens—
the only city in Hellas willing to take us in.
Come, boys, give your hands to these men of Athens,
(*gently pushing* SONS *toward* CHORUS, *and beckoning to*
individual choristers)
and you, gentlemen, give them your hands.
                              —Boys,
we've tested this city's friendship.   320
Now, if someday you see your home in Argos again;

if someday you inherit your father's house and honors,
remember Athens, remember these friends.
They saved your lives. Think of this day,
and swear eternal peace between yourselves and Athens.
These men have earned your loyalty, your love.
They readily accepted the burdens we brought with us,
even the vengeance of the Argives.
Remember what they did.
They saw we were helpless exiles, wanderers,   330
but refused to surrender us or drive us out.
(*to* DEMOPHON) In life, and in death, when at last I come
   to die,
I'll honor your name, my lord Demophon. And when at
   last
I stand with Theseus, I'll bring him news to make him
   proud,
proud to hear how courageously you welcomed
and protected the sons of Herakles,
how splendidly you upheld his fame and honor.
You are your father's son, Demophon, no less great than he
in nature, in action. Most men are faint reflections
of their fathers. Sons like you are rare, King Demophon.   340

LEADER Athens has always defended the oppressed
when their cause was just. For friends like these
we have suffered greatly in the past.
Now another trial lies before us.

DEMOPHON (*to* IOLAOS) Well spoken, sir. I know that these boys
will remember your words, and the actions of Athens.
Now I'll go and mobilize the citizens
so I can meet the Argive attack with my forces
fully mustered. I don't want to be caught off guard,
so first I'll send out scouts to reconnoiter.   350
Count on it—the Argives are disciplined and ready.
Then I'll have the priests prepare the sacrifice.
You, Iolaos, leave the altar and go to my house.
My servants will take care of you while I'm away.
(IOLAOS *does not move*) Go inside, old friend.

41

IOLAOS I'd rather stay here, here at the altar. Let us stay
where we can offer prayers for the city's success.
We'll join you inside after the Argives are defeated.
(DEMOPHON *hesitates*)
My lord, now we have gods to call upon, gods as great
as any gods of Argos. Hera is their champion; ours   360
is Athena. Success means having stronger gods,
and honoring their strength—or so I hold.
Goddess Athena will never know defeat.

Exit DEMOPHON. IOLAOS *and the* SONS *assemble at the altar.*
A trumpet sounds.

LEADER Boast away.
What do we care for your bluster?

CHORUS (*speaking individually*)
—Your Argos is nothing here, stranger.
—You won't frighten me with your bragging threats.
—This is Athens. —This great city
has no fear of you.

LEADER Not Athens,   370
where the wheeling chorus
weaves the lovely mazes of the dance.

CHORUS (*speaking individually*)
—You're mad.
—Mad as your master, Eurystheus of Argos.
—You come to a city as great as Argos—

LEADER You lay violent hands on helpless wanderers
who sought asylum here
at the altars of our gods.

CHORUS (*speaking individually*)
—You flouted our king's authority.
—Offered no justification.   380
—How can such arrogant madness win approval

from sane and prudent men?
—We are peace-loving people.

                      —And now, herald,
take our message home to your lunatic master:

LEADER Tell Eurystheus this: King,
if in your rage, your frenzied anger,
you think to seize this city,
I warn you: It will not be,
nothing will happen as you dream.

CHORUS (*speaking individually*)
  —There are swords in Athens too,   390
Athens has shields of shining bronze.
  —You love war, you and your Argos.
  —But keep your lust for war, your turmoil,
  —keep them to yourselves, keep them at home in Argos.
  —Here, they have no place, they are strangers here,
  —here where the Graces live,
  —at peace, at peace in shining Athens.
  —King, in the name of the graces, then:
  —hold back.

Enter DEMOPHON, *accompanied by three or four armed*
                                   men.

IOLAOS What is it, son? You must have news   400
of the enemy. I can see it in your eyes.
Are they on the move, or already here?
That herald of his wasn't simply bragging.
The gods have always smiled upon Eurystheus,
and now, glowing with confidence, he's marching here,
where Zeus, who punishes all arrogance of mortal thought,
will bring him down.

DEMOPHON   The Argives are here,
Eurystheus at their head. Rather than rely on scouts,
I observed them at first hand, with my own eyes,

so I can give responsible orders to our army.   410
The enemy hasn't moved to occupy the plain. Instead,
Eurystheus has taken a temporary position
on high ground, along the ridge. He'll be looking,
I think, for the safest means of bringing his troops down
before making camp in Attika. And we'll be ready for them.
The city's fully mustered. The sacrifices
have been prepared as required by the gods receiving them.
Everywhere in Athens the priests have made offerings
intended to repel the enemy and save the city.
I've summoned all the seers; I've questioned them,   420
every prophetic voice in Athens, about the ancient oracles—
those in common domain, those that circulate in secret.
No detail bearing on our safety has been omitted.
In many small matters, the oracles disagree,
but in one essential point, Iolaos, they all concur.
They command me to sacrifice to Persephone. To sacrifice
a virgin, a girl of noble birth.

    You know the good will I bear you, Iolaos, but this new
requirement is too much. I will not kill my own daughter,
nor will I compel any Athenian to such an act   430
against his will. What man would be so mad
as to kill his own child? Now, all over the city,
people are gathered in small groups, arguing whether
we ought to protect the suppliants, or whether I'm mad
in promising to help you. If I order such a sacrifice,
civil war will be the consequence.
So now I need your help. Help me find some way
of saving you, these children, and this city,
without subjecting me to the city's bitter anger.
I am no tyrant, no barbarian.   440
If I act fairly, others will be fair with me.

LEADER   Are the gods opposed to helping these strangers?

IOLAOS   Poor children, we're like sailors at sea.
They escape the savage anger of the gale,
they reach out to touch the land, and an offshore wind,

gusting hard, drives them back out to sea again.
That's how it is with us—driven from this land
when we were almost there, safe ashore, or so we thought.
Hope, hope. Why was I allowed the joy of hoping
only to have its promise torn from my hands?   450
I understand Demophon's decision not to kill
his people's children. He has done what he could—
and should. My lord, even if the gods oppose me,
my gratitude to you remains the same.

                —Boys, I don't know what to do.
Where can we turn? Is there any god we haven't invoked?
Where haven't we turned for shelter and protection?
We'll be surrendered to Argos, and we'll die.
My life doesn't count, doesn't matter,
except that by dying I delight my enemies.
It's you I pity, boys—   460
you and your old grandmother, Alkmene.
Poor woman, to have lived so long, only to come to
     this . . .
I pity you, pity myself—all my sufferings and trials,
all for nothing.

               No way out.
We were fated to fall into Eurystheus' hands,
fated to die in dishonor and shame.
(to DEMOPHON) No, wait. There's still a chance, one
     chance,
of saving these boys. You can help me, Demophon.
Surrender me to the Argives in their place.
You risk nothing, and the boys will be safe.   470
To have Herakles' friend in his power—to humiliate me—
there's nothing Eurystheus would like more.
The man is brutal. Civilized men should pray
for enemies like themselves, not brute savages.
Then, even in defeat, there'd be respect,
there'd be compassion.

LEADER Old sir, your suggestion dishonors this city.
        The charge of failure to defend a suppliant

is false, yet it's a shameful accusation.
It brings disgrace.   480

DEMOPHON Noble words, but no solution.
It's not for you Eurystheus brings his army here.
What does Eurystheus gain from an old man's death?
He wants to kill these boys. Why not?
They're the sons of Herakles. They're nobly born;
grown to manhood, they'd be bound to avenge their
            father's wrongs.
They'd be dangerous to him. Eurystheus knows that;
he has to act before it happens. Now,
if you have some better idea, some effective plan,
let me hear it. For my part,   490
I've seen the oracles; and I'm afraid.

MAKARIA *appears in the temple doorway, and pauses before*
                    approaching IOLAOS. *She is about fifteen.*

MAKARIA Strangers, please don't think my coming out
is brashness. I ask your pardon. I know
that women are honored most for silence, for knowing
and keeping their proper place at home.
But when I heard that anguish in your voice, Iolaos,
I couldn't stay inside. I had to come out.
I'm not head of this family, I know that.
Still, I should be here. I love my brothers.
I'm here for them. For them, for myself,   500
I have to know what's happened.

IOLAOS Daughter, of all the children of Herakles, it's you
I've always admired the most. And how right I was.
Just when I thought all was well, suddenly
everything turned hopeless. According to King Demophon,
the oracles demand a living human sacrifice.
Not a bull, no sheep, but a girl, a virgin
of noble birth must be sacrificed to Persephone
in order to save this city and ourselves. There's no
            other way,

no way out. Demophon refuses absolutely   510
to sacrifice his own child, or any other man's.
Either we must extricate ourselves on our own,
or we seek asylum elsewhere. Those aren't his exact words,
but the meaning is clear. His first priority
is the safety of Athens.

MAKARIA   Then our lives depend
        upon this sacrifice?

IOLAOS   Yes, provided other things go well.

MAKARIA Then you needn't fear the Argives any more.
        I'll be your sacrifice. Unforced, of my own free will,
        I volunteer my life.
        (*stopping* IOLAOS' *protest*) The people of Athens have   520
                risked their lives for us.
        So how can we, who imposed our burdens on them,
        shrink from dying, when by our dying we give them
        life? What could we say in our defense?
        Not a word.
                        It would be cowardice, contemptible,
        if we who, weeping, sought asylum at the altars of their
                gods,
        who boast ourselves to be the children of Herakles,
        should cringe from death. Every decent man
        would laugh us to scorn.
                        No, far better
        this city should fall—the gods forbid!—   530
        better the enemy should take me prisoner, treat me
        with outrage and abuse me, daughter of a hero though
                I am,
        and, in the end, send me down to Hades just the same.
        And what if I'm banished?
        What could I say for shame when people ask me
        why I come to them with suppliant branches, imploring
                their help,
        but show a coward's love of life? They'd drive me out,
        saying, "Cowards get no sanctuary here."

And suppose my brothers die, leaving me
alive, alone, what hope of happiness would I have?
Many men have sacrificed family and friends   540
to their own happiness. I couldn't do it.
Who would want a wife without family or friends?
What man would want my children? Better, far better,
    to die
than live so empty a life. It might suit
another woman, but it will not do for me.
I am my father's daughter.
                  I am ready.
Take me to the place of sacrifice,
wreathe my head with garlands, perform your rite.
Then go fight. Fight and win. Of my own free will,
unforced, I give my life. Tell the world   550
I'm dying for my brothers, I'm dying for myself.
It's not life, not my life, that matters.
And knowing that, I've found a better thing
than life itself, by bravely leaving it.

LEADER   What can I say to such noble words—
this girl's offer to die for her brothers?
No man could speak so well or act so bravely.

IOLAOS   Your spirit reveals your birth.
You are the true daughter of your father Herakles,
son of highest Zeus. I'm proud of you, proud
of your words, but there's bitterness in what you say.   560
Let me propose a fairer solution:
we'll ask your sisters to come outside,
we'll draw lots. The sister chosen will die
on behalf of her brothers. It's the fairest thing
to decide the issue by lot.

MAKARIA   I refuse to let my death depend on chance.
It has no grace of freedom. Not another word.
If you accept my offer, if you stand ready
to make use of me, I am ready, of my own free will,
unforced, to give my brothers the gift of my life.   570

IOLAOS Dearest child.
Your earlier words were unsurpassable,
but these words surpass them. In bravery,
in generosity, you outdo even yourself. I cannot order
you to die, I can't prevent it. But by dying
you save your brothers' lives.

MAKARIA   You speak wisely.
Don't fear my death will taint you. I die of my own free
    will.
    But go with me, Iolaos. Be there to hold me
when I die, cover my body with my dress.
My father was Herakles, but I'm still afraid. I need you   580
    there
beside me, Iolaos, when I face the knife.

IOLAOS I couldn't bear it, standing beside you, watching
you die.

MAKARIA   Then ask the king to see to it
that I die with women around me, not men.

DEMOPHON Granted. I pity you. It would be disgrace and shame
for me to refuse you these last honors
so clearly required by your generosity, your bravery,
and what is right. I have never seen,
never, a woman of greater courage. Now,
if you have any last words for your brothers   590
and Iolaos, speak, child. It's time to go.

MAKARIA Goodbye, old friend. Farewell.
                              Teach these brothers of mine
to be like you. Make them wise and kind
in everything, like you. That's all; I want nothing more.
Protect them. Cherish them. I know how well
you love them. We're your children. You cared for us,
you brought us up. And now you see me go
unmarried, to death, dying for my brothers
clustered here around me.
                              —Brothers, I wish you

600

all success and happiness, every good thing
of which my death deprives me.
                              Honor Iolaos, honor
your grandmother, Alkmene. Honor these men of Athens.
And if someday the gods send you release
from your wanderings and give you back your home
in Argos, remember me, remember the funeral honors
due the sister who saved you.
                              Let my honors match
my gift: I stood at your side when you needed me,
I gave my life for you.
                         In the place of children
I will never have, these are all my treasures,
these are my reward,
                         if anything goes with us underground.   610
Nothingness is best. If even after death
we endure the troubles which burden us here on earth,
there's no escape. For human suffering,
the strongest medicine, I think, is death.

IOLAOS Generous, courageous girl, you are the noblest
        woman I have ever known. Living and dying,
        you will have our reverence and honor, always.
        Farewell . . . I am afraid to speak ill-omened
        words of goddess Persephone, to whom your body
        is consecrated.

                Exit MAKARIA, *escorted by* DEMOPHON.

                         Boys, this is too much,   620
too much pain, I need to sit . . .
Help me rest my back
against the altar. Cover my head with my robes.

                SONS *place* IOLAOS' *cloak over his head.*

This is a cruel deliverance.
We had this choice: to obey the oracle, or die.

Your death would have been a worse grief even than this,
but the choice we made is anguish, torture.

CHORUS (*speaking individually*)—Man's mind and hands, without
              the gods, can devise no triumph—not even failure.
        —Success vanishes, does not return.
        —Will not grow again in the same field,   630
              will not return with the seasons.
        —One fortune crowds out another, uprooting
              a man from his place in the sun,
              planting him again in stony darkness.
        —Or suddenly veers, shifting direction—
              as when a poor man stumbles on shining gold.
        —The gods hold us, caught fast in the torrent.
        —The man who tries to change the course of this current
              by stubbornness, by craft,
              struggles in vain.   640

        —Bear your burden.
        —Whatever the gods may send, do not falter.
              Endure it, unembittered.
        —Even as she dies, this girl discovers
              deathless honor and glory in giving her life
              for her brothers, for us all.
        —The glory she leaves behind her will shine forever,
              as noble actions outshine the darkest pain.
        —What she does today is worthy of her birth,
              worthy of her father Herakles.   650
        —Whoever you may be, if you kneel in reverence
              for human bravery;
        —if you kneel in honor of nobility, and in
              sorrow at its dying;
        —you will find me here, kneeling at your side,
                              (*the speaker of this line kneels*)
        —as I kneel now.

        Enter SERVANT *of Hyllos. He does not at first see* IOLAOS.

SERVANT Boys, where are Iolaos and Alkmene?
         Have they left the altar?

IOLAOS Here I am—what's left of me.

SERVANT Why are you sitting there, staring at the ground?   660

IOLAOS Sorrow for this family. Grief.

SERVANT Stand up. Lift your head.

IOLAOS I am too old, too old. I have no strength.

SERVANT My news is good news.

IOLAOS Who are you?
        Do I know you? I can't remember.

SERVANT Hyllos' servant. You know me now?

IOLAOS Welcome, friend. Good news, you say?

SERVANT Glorious news.

IOLAOS (calling toward the temple) Alkmene, come outside!   670
            I have good news!
        (to SERVANT) Poor terrified woman. She's the mother of
            Herakles,
        and yet a lifetime of concern for Hyllos and the other
            children
        has nearly broken her.

        Enter ALKMENE from the temple. She is a very old woman,
                            darkly and shabbily dressed.

ALKMENE Why all this shouting, Iolaos?
         Is this another herald? With more threats?
         (to SERVANT) I'm a weak old woman, stranger, but I
             warn you,

52

touch these children, you'll have to kill me first,
or I'm not the mother of Herakles. Touch them,
and you'll have a shameful struggle with two old people.

IOLAOS Stop, Alkmene. Don't be afraid.   680
This is no herald bringing threats from Argos.

ALKMENE Your shouting frightened me.

IOLAOS I was calling you to come out and see him.

ALKMENE I don't understand. See who?

IOLAOS A messenger. He says that Hyllos is back.

ALKMENE (to SERVANT) Then welcome, friend! You and your
            news are welcome.
        But where is Hyllos? I want him.
        Why isn't he here?

SERVANT He's reviewing his troops, assigning them their positions.

ALKMENE I don't understand these military matters.   690

IOLAOS I do. Tell me.

SERVANT What do you want to know?

IOLAOS How large is the allied force under Hyllos' command?

SERVANT Strong. I don't know the exact number.

IOLAOS The Athenian generals have been informed?

SERVANT Yes. They've stationed Hyllos on the left flank.

IOLAOS Is the army drawn up in battle formation?

SERVANT Drawn up, and the sacrifice is ready.
        The animals have been driven up to the front lines.

53

IOLAOS How near is the Argive army?   700

SERVANT Near enough so we could see Eurystheus clearly.

IOLAOS What was he doing? Marshalling his men?

SERVANT I think so. We couldn't hear the words.
But I must go, sir. I can't desert my commander.
Not when the battle's about to begin.

IOLAOS We think alike. I'm going with you. Friends help friends.

SERVANT Sir, this is no time for foolishness.

IOLAOS Foolishness? To fight in my own cause?

SERVANT Sir, you're not the man you used to be.

IOLAOS I'm still man enough to handle a spear.   710

SERVANT Man enough—provided you don't stumble.

IOLAOS One look at me, and the Argives will take cover.

SERVANT Looks don't draw blood, sir. I wish they did.

IOLAOS If I go, that's one more man on our side.
That changes the odds.

SERVANT Not very much.

IOLAOS Enough talk. It's time for action.

SERVANT Action, sir? Wishing would be more like it.

IOLAOS Call it what you like. I'm on my way.

SERVANT How can you fight without armor?   720

IOLAOS There's captured armor hanging on the temple walls.
I'll use that. If I live, I'll return it.
If I die, the god won't want it back.
Take it off the pegs and bring it here.

Exit SERVANT

Only a coward would stay here, safe behind walls,
while others do our fighting for us.

Members of the CHORUS *approach* IOLAOS *and speak individually to him.*

CHORUS —Time has not weakened your spirit.
Your will is as young as ever.
—But your body, your strength, are gone.
—Why these useless efforts,   730
these struggles to help our cause?
—They only hurt you,
    and do our cause no good.
Remember your age. Let these fantasies go.
—Your youth is gone. —Your strength is gone.
—Gone forever.

ALKMENE Have you lost your mind, Iolaos?
Are you deserting me and these children?

IOLAOS War is man's work. You mind the young.

ALKMENE But if you die, what will become of me?

IOLAOS Your grandchildren will take good care of you.   740

ALKMENE But what if something should happen to them?

IOLAOS The Athenians will protect you. Don't be afraid.

ALKMENE Then they're my only protection, my only hope.

IOLAOS Zeus knows your troubles. Zeus cares.

ALKMENE Zeus?
          Zeus will never hear a word of reproach from my lips,
          but Zeus knows best how he's treated me.

          ALKMENE sits on a corner of the altar-base as the SERVANT
                              returns from the temple, carrying armor.

SERVANT Here's your armor. Quick, on with it.
          The battle's begun. Ares hates a straggler.

                      IOLAOS struggles unsuccessfully with the armor.

          Let it be. If it's too heavy, go as you are.   750
          Put it on when we reach the ranks. I'll carry it.

IOLAOS Good. Carry it, but keep it handy.
          Now put the spear in my hand. Take my arm. There.
          Brace me. Steady, steady.

SERVANT Are you a soldier, or a schoolboy?

IOLAOS Don't let me stumble. A bad omen.

SERVANT I wish your legs could match your zeal.

                                              They begin to move off.

IOLAOS Move! I don't want to miss the fight.

SERVANT Move, is it? You only imagine you're moving.

IOLAOS Can't you see how fast I'm going?   760

SERVANT The speed is all in your mind.

IOLAOS Wait till you see me in action.

SERVANT Action, you say.

> IOLAOS *stumbles; the* SERVANT *holds him up.*

> I wish you luck, sir.

IOLAOS I'll split their shields, I'll shatter them!

SERVANT If we ever get there. Which I doubt.

> IOLAOS *stops.*

IOLAOS Oh, gods, give me back
the strength of this good right arm of mine!
Make me what I was when I was young
and at Herakles' side, I took the city of Sparta!
Give me back my youth, let me crush that coward   770
Eurystheus now. He couldn't face my spear.
When men succeed, we wrongly assume they're brave;
we wrongly think they're clever.

> Exit IOLAOS *and* SERVANT. *The* CHORUS, *from watching them
> go, turn toward the audience, looking above and beyond it.*

CHORUS Now may earth, and the nightlong moon, and sunlight
shafts of the shining god whose radiance reaches down,
touching all mortals, be our messengers.
Let the word go soaring up to the high throne,
and echo through gray-eyed Athena's halls:
We're ready, ready to take up shining steel, ready to fight
for these guests of ours, for Athens,   780
        for glory, and home.

Oh, day of shame when Mykenai,
arrogant in her swelling power,
came breathing hatred against our city.
And this too, oh Athens, would be a thing of shame,
to drive away these suppliants at Mykenai's demand.
Our ally is Zeus. We are not afraid.

Zeus will be just with us; and we, in what we do,
will make his meaning clear: no mortal power
    can compete with god.   790

Lady Athena, this land, this city, are yours.
You are our mother, our mistress, our shield.
Rout the arrogance of Argos! Drive this army
far from this holy place! Our justice, our courage deserve
their home, deserve to hold and keep this land forever.
Great Athena, honor and sacrifice have always been yours.
Our city remembers always the waning of the moon,
when songs of children rise and chanting voices
glorify your name, and on your windy rock
voices lift in praise, with the sound of maidens dancing   800
as the bright moon sets toward morning.

Enter MESSENGER, *a slave of* ALKMENE.

MESSENGER Mistress, my message is brief and glorious.
    We have beaten our enemies, their armor is our trophy.

ALKMENE Then you're welcome! Welcome. For bringing me this
        news,
    dear friend, I give you your freedom. Now free me
    from my fears. Is Hyllos alive?

MESSENGER Alive, and acclaimed a hero.

ALKMENE And Iolaos, is he alive?

MESSENGER More than alive. Thanks to the gods, he performed
    miracles.

ALKMENE Iolaos? You mean he fought bravely?   810

MESSENGER No, it was a miracle, lady.
    There he was, an old man. And suddenly he was young
    again.

ALKMENE A miracle indeed, if true.

But tell me first about the battle
and how it went. I want to hear how our men won.

MESSENGER I'll tell you the whole story, from start to finish. Listen:
There we were, drawn up in battle formation, each
army ready, impatient to get at the other.
Then Hyllos, dismounting from his chariot, walked out
alone, the spears bristling all around him,
and shouted to the Argive king: 820
"I challenge you, Eurystheus. Leave this land at peace.
Why risk hurting Argos, or any Argive soldier?
Meet me yourself, alone, in single combat.
Kill me, and the sons of Herakles are yours
to do with what you will. But if you lose, give me
back my father's honors. Give me back my country."
Men on both sides cheered. They heard a brave man
speaking, and they saw a way to avoid
a terrible battle.
But nothing could shame Eurystheus, nothing.   830
There he stood, the supreme Argive commander, proven
a coward in the presence of thousands
of watching soldiers,
and still he refused to accept Hyllos' brave
and generous challenge.
And this is the man—this proven coward—who
wants to capture the sons of Herakles!
So Hyllos returned to his place in the ranks,
and the priests, knowing that the battle was inevitable,
swiftly sacrificed the victims   840
and drew the human blood whose shedding made
our victory certain.
Then the cavalry mounted their chariots,
the foot soldiers raised their shields,
lapping them together into a wall of iron.
The king of Athens addressed his army
as though he had been born a general:
"Fellow Citizens, this mother earth that gave you life,

this sacred earth of Attika that nourishes us all,
 now summons you to her defense!"   850
On the other side, Eurystheus implored his troops
 not to disgrace Argos and Mykenai.
The trumpets sounded the charge, and the massed armies
 crashed against each other. Lady,
try to imagine it—the clanging of metal shields,
 and the sudden, final cries of dying men!
First, the shock of the Argive charge broke our ranks;
 then the Argives pulled back. Then, toe to toe,
 in the second charge,
they fought hand to hand, desperately, and many   860
 brave soldiers died.
You could hear men shouting from both sides:
 "Hold on, men of Athens!" "Sons of Argos, charge!"
 "Save your country from disgrace!"
At last, with all our strength, with heavy losses,
 we drove them from the battlefield.
Then, suddenly, Hyllos' chariot broke through the lines.
 Iolaos hailed him down and begged to have
 the chariot for himself.
So Iolaos picked up the reins and drove, fast and hard,   870
 straight after Eurystheus.
That much I saw myself, but I only heard reports
 about what happened next.
Iolaos had just passed Athena's sacred hill at Pallene
 when he saw Eurystheus' chariot ahead,
and he prayed aloud, to Zeus and Hebe, asking
 to have his youth restored for this one day,
 so he could take revenge on his old enemy.
Now, this was the miracle:
Suddenly, two stars, all blazing fire, settle down   880
 on the horses' yokes, hiding the chariot
 in a kind of cloud, or shadow.
Men who understand these things said those stars
 were Hebe and your son, Herakles.
Then, out of that darkness in the air came Iolaos—
 young, his strong shoulders straining on the reins,

a man in all the vigor and freshness of his youth.
There, right by the rocks of Skiron, he caught his man
    and threw him into chains. Now,
    he is bringing Eurystheus here—   890
Eurystheus himself, once a king, the greatest man
    in Argos, almost a god; now, nothing at all,
    a prisoner of war, a man in chains.
The meaning is clear, lady, clear to all who see.
No human fortune lasts. Glory dies, greatness fades.
Call no man happy until he dies.

LEADER   Oh, Zeus,
god of victory, now I see the dawning day
whose sunlight sets me free of fear at last!

ALKMENE Oh, Zeus, you took your time, watching me suffer.
Still, I give you thanks for what has happened here.   900
I never really believed my son had become a god
among the gods in heaven. But now I know it's true.
    At last you boys will be free of your trials,
at last you'll be free of that damned tyrant,
Eurystheus. You will see your father's native city
of Argos, you will walk your native earth again,
    make sacrifice to your father's ancestral gods,
all those good things from which you've been excluded,
    boys,
to live as fugitives, your wandering unhappy lives.
(to MESSENGER) But why did Iolaos spare Eurystheus' life?   910
What was his real purpose?
                   Answer me.
It makes no sense to me to take your enemy
and not take your revenge.

MESSENGER   He was thinking of you.
He wanted you to see Eurystheus yourself—
see him subject to your will, your slave.
Eurystheus, of course, resisted—so they used
force, they yoked him. He had no wish

to meet your eyes and suffer your revenge.
And now, lady, I take my leave. Remember
what you said when I started to speak—   920
that you would set me free. In matters like this,
noble tongues should keep their word.

Exit MESSENGER. *Slowly and reverently, as the* LEADER
speaks, the CHORUS *assemble to offer a prayer of gratitude.*

LEADER Sweet, the dance is sweet when with it comes
the high, clear song of the flute,
and goddess Aphrodite graces the feast.

CHORUS But sweeter than all dancing
is the coming on of good fortune, against all
        expectation,
touching the lives of those we love.
All things come to pass, all converges at the touch of Fate,
and the strong persistence of Time.   930

LEADER Oh, city, honoring the gods, your road is justice.
Never leave this path.

CHORUS Who could say of Athens
that she swerved from the path of justice? Only a fool
        could say it,
given the vindication of this day. Always, always
the gods curb the high ambitions of arrogant men, always
they make their meaning clear, for all to see.

LEADER The story is true, lady. Your Herakles is a god.

CHORUS They lied, they lied, who said
that Herakles descended to the world below,   940
his body consumed in the agony of fire.
With Hebe at his side
in a bed of shining gold, he lives forever in the golden
        house
of his father Zeus, and Hymenaios joins two gods in love.

LEADER All things converge at last. This is the pattern.

CHORUS They say Athena once appeared
        and rescued Herakles. And now,
        in turn, this Athens of the goddess
        has saved the sons of Herakles
        and mastered a man who chose not justice but violence.   950
        May such passionate ambition never be mine.

        Enter Hyllos' SERVANT *from the right, with two spearmen
        who escort* EURYSTHEUS *in chains, his upper arms bound
        to a yoke across his shoulders.*

SERVANT Mistress, you can see for yourself, but give me the joy
             of saying:
         we've brought you Eurystheus. There he is.
         A sight you never thought to see. No more
         than he ever dreamed of being your prisoner,
         when, with such huge effort and expense, breathing
         arrogance, outraging justice, he marched from Argos
         to destroy Athens. But the gods prevented him,
         opposing his ambition, reversing his hopes.   960
         In gratitude for victory, Hyllos and brave Iolaos
         have set up an image of Zeus—Zeus of Victory.
         They commanded me to bring Eurystheus here,
         to delight your eyes. There's no sweeter sight
         than to see the enemy you hate in failure and defeat,
         reduced to nothing.

ALKMENE   Monster, is it really you?
        Has justice found you out at last?
        Turn your head and look me straight
        in the face. You hate me? Then look at me,
             monster.

        Spearmen grasp yoke and twist EURYSTHEUS' *face toward*
                                                    ALKMENE.

63

You're *my* slave now, *I* am the master. 970
Are you the same Eurystheus—I can't believe it—
the same Eurystheus who persecuted my son—
wherever he is now—with outrage on outrage?
Was any outrage too much for you, monster?
You sent a living man down to Hades,
you dispatched him all over the world, made him kill
hydras and lions and—but I can't count out
all your atrocities.
                    And even that wasn't enough.
You hounded me, you hounded these poor children
all over Hellas. Young and old alike, 980
you made us seek asylum at the gods' altars
everywhere. But here in Athens you found
a free city, free men who weren't afraid of you.
And now you'll die as you deserve—a slave's death,
and still come out ahead. You ought to die not once,
but over and over and over. I want to see you die
one death for every wrong and cruelty you committed.

SERVANT But you can't put him to death. Not now.

ALKMENE Why else take him prisoner?
         What law prevents me from putting this man to death? 990

SERVANT The Athenian authorities. They won't allow it.

ALKMENE Won't *allow* it?
         Since when is it wrong to kill your enemies?

SERVANT When your enemies are prisoners of war.

ALKMENE Hyllos agreed to *that?*

SERVANT You want him to disobey the law of Athens?

ALKMENE Eurystheus deserves death. He has no right to live.

SERVANT Then we were wrong to take him prisoner.

ALKMENE Why is it wrong to punish him?

LEADER You won't find anyone to execute him now.   1000

ALKMENE I'm your anyone. *I'll* kill him.

LEADER The whole city will condemn you.

ALKMENE I love this city, who dares say I don't?
But now that this man has fallen into my hands,
no power on earth can take him from me.
Call me what you like, call me cruel,
say I'm more arrogant than woman ought to be—
but this man *must* die, and *I* will do it.

LEADER I know how bitterly you hate this man,
Alkmene. I know, I understand your feelings.   1010

EURYSTHEUS I refuse to grovel at your feet, woman,
or beg you for my life. I won't say one word
to vindicate your charge of cowardice.
I didn't choose this feud of my own free will.
I know that you and I are cousins,
that I'm related by blood to your son, Herakles.
But whether I chose this feud or not, it wasn't I
but the goddess Hera. She yoked me
with this sickness, this affliction. And once our contest
had begun, once I knew I had to persevere   1020
and fight it to the bitter end, I started planning,
scheming. Night after night I stared into the dark,
plotting to get rid of my enemies and destroy them.
I couldn't live my days and nights in terror.
And I knew your son was no cipher, but a man,
a real man. I hated him, but he was great,
a hero—I admit it. When he died,
what choice did I have? His sons hated me;
in them the father's feud remained alive.
I couldn't leave one stone unturned—murder, banishment,   1030

plots, anything at all, anything to end my fears.
If you had been there in my place, how would you
have acted? Would you have ignored these vicious cubs?
Oh, you would have been more humane, you
would have let them grow up and inherit Argos,
wouldn't you? Absurd.
                          So,
since I didn't die on the field of battle,
where I wanted to die, how do matters stand?
By all Greek law, a prisoner's person is sacred.
My death defiles my killer, it becomes a curse.   1040
This was why Athens, wisely, spared me, believing
in respect for heaven, not mindless revenge.

       You have my answer, woman. Count on it,
if you kill me, I'll take my revenge on you—
the noble vengeance of the dead.
This is how it stands with me: I have no wish to die;
and no great passion to go on living.

LEADER Alkmene, my advice to you is this:
  do not harm this man. Athens has spared him.
  Respect that decision.   1050

ALKMENE But suppose he dies, and at the same time,
  I respect the city's decision.

LEADER That would be best, but how can it be?

ALKMENE Simplicity itself. I put him to death,
  then surrender his body to those who come to claim it.
  Where his body is concerned, I obey the city.
  But he dies, and by dying, pays his debt to me.

EURYSTHEUS Kill me. I don't want mercy.
  But since Athens spared me, rightly and humanely
  refusing to kill a prisoner, I now offer this city   1060
  my gift, an ancient oracle of Apollo,
  which in time to come will prove a far greater blessing

than anyone now dreams. Bury my body in the place
    decreed
by Fate, before Athena's shrine at Pallene.
There, an honored guest of state beneath the Attic earth,
I will keep this city safe, forever.
                            And in future years,
when these children's children forget your kindness
and the gratitude they owe you, returning
as armed invaders, I will be their bitter enemy. Traitors,
ingrates—these are the guests you championed.   1070
Why, knowing this, did I choose to ignore the warning
of the oracle, and lead my army here to Athens?
Because I believed the goddess Hera was stronger
than any oracle, that she would stand by my side.
Pour no libations of wine or blood upon my grave.
Let it be, and I will give these children's children
a bitter homecoming. You profit doubly from my death.
It will be a blessing to Athens, and a curse on them.

ALKMENE (*to* CHORUS) What are you waiting for? You heard his
    prophecy.
Put him to death, and you assure your city's safety.   1080
Kill him. Now.
He shows you where your safety lies.
Alive, he's your enemy; dead, your ally, your friend.
Take him away, men. Kill him!
Throw his body to the dogs!
(*to* EURYSTHEUS)   Dead,
you'll never drive me from my father's land again.

CHORUS We agree.
Guards, take him away.
By our actions here,
our kings are innocent.   1090

ALL *exit;* ALKMENE *and the* SONS *first, then the* CHORUS *and
the* SERVANT. EURYSTHEUS *and the spearmen are left; they
    move slowly off after the others.*

NOTES AND GLOSSARY

NOTES

The physical setting of the *Children of Herakles* is in Attika and would therefore be entirely familiar to the Athenian audience. Euripides fills the play with references to the topography of Attika and its neighboring lands, with a specific dramatic intention.

The scene is at Marathon, about twenty-three miles by road northeast of Athens. The marshy plain between Marathon and the sea was the place where the Athenians defeated the Persian army in 490 B.C. In the prologue and the first episode of the play the action, taking place before the temple of Zeus at Marathon, is continuous. It concludes with the departure of Kopreus, the Argive herald, then of Demophon to mobilize the Athenians. Between the first and second episodes, however, and between each succeeding pair of episodes in the play, much action takes place which in normal time would require days or weeks to accomplish. The audience's knowledge of the geographic setting would bring this to their minds, and would reinforce the sense of rapid motion and the pressure of events which is already implicit in the play.

Between the first and second episodes the herald reaches the Megarian frontier from Marathon, some fifty miles away. Eurystheus marches his army into Attika and takes up his position on a mountain overlooking Marathon (probably Mt. Brilessos), a distance of about forty miles. Meanwhile Demophon is mobilizing the Athenians from the other towns in Attika, bringing them to Marathon, preparing sacrifices, and inquiring and receiving responses from the oracles.

Between the second and the third episodes, Hyllos arrives at Marathon with an army collected outside Attika, and joins the Athenian forces. The Argives descend to the plain, and both armies array themselves for battle.

Between the third and fourth episodes the battle is fought, and the Argives are defeated. Iolaos pursues Eurystheus via Pallene, past Athens and Megara, to the Skironian rocks, a distance of over sixty miles, captures him and dispatches him back to Marathon.

Between the fourth and fifth episodes Eurystheus completes his journey to Marathon. The Athenian rulers decide that his life must be spared.

The impression of the play against its physical background is that of a swift and vivid chronicle. Each episode represents a reaction by the characters to a new and changed situation. Between the episodes the choral odes are suspended in a time-movement which is different from that of the dramatic action.

NOTES ON THE TEXT

9 *the bond of blood* Iolaos was traditionally Herakles' nephew, and served him as charioteer and shieldbearer in his adventures. See the genealogical table at the note to 213. Since Iolaos in the play is much older than would be possible for the nephew of Herakles, Euripides does not mention a specific kin-relationship between the two here or elsewhere in the play.

13 *under the dwindling shadow of my wings* Aeschylus had used the phrase as a metaphor for the divine protection of Athens and its citizens by Athena (*Eumenides*, 1001). The Euripidean character repeats it with conscious irony.

39-40 *when the descendants of Pandion/divided the kingdom* Choice of certain civic officers, such as archons, by lot was a feature of fifth-century Athenian democracy. The origin of the practice was often referred to the heroic age, in this case to the descendants of Pandion, the great-grandfather of Demophon and Akamas. See the genealogy at the note to 213.

56 *mouthing your demands* Kopreus had been Eurystheus' agent in commanding Herakles to undertake his twelve labors.

74 *Men of Athens!* Iolaos' cry for help incorporates an allusion that is not translatable. Literally he says: "You who have lived in Athens too long

a time." The Athenians prided themselves on being autochthonous, that is, on having been the original inhabitants of Attika, rather than migrants from elsewhere. Iolaos is saying with his characteristic ironic force that they have lived too long in one place—that is, they have become senseless clods—if they can allow such outrages to happen.

77-121 Entrance of the Chorus: The Chorus enter hastily, and it is clear from the language that more than one member of the group speaks (77-81). We have assigned these lines alternately to the leader and to a second leader of the Chorus, following with some variation the attribution of the Budé editor. We have then continued the participation of the second leader in the dialogue until the entrance of Demophon and Akamas (122). The Budé editor assigns all the Chorus' lines after 82 to the leader alone.

85 *How did you get to Marathon?* The Greek refers to the Tetrapolis, an ancient confederation of four neighboring Attic towns: Marathon, Trikory-thos, Probalinthos, and Oinoe. See the geographic note, p. 71.

112 The editor of the Budé text suggests that some verses have disappeared between this and the next line.

120 *Akamas* He was Demophon's brother and shared the kingship with him after Theseus' death. His entrance is puzzling, since he has no words to say and no function in the play. It may be that the tradition of this dual kingship was strong enough at Athens so that the audience would expect to see both. The twin Dioskuri, Kastor and Polydeukes, appear in Euripides' *Helen*, but only one speaks. We have indicated Akamas' departure after Kopreus' scene, but a modern production of the play would not suffer if he were removed entirely.

136 *King Eurystheus* Kopreus deliberately insults Demophon in this speech. Although he has been told that Demophon is king of Athens, and has reserved his arguments for the supreme authority, he recognizes only Eurystheus as "king" and addresses Demophon as "sir" (138).

140 *to take formal custody of Argive runaways* Kopreus uses a term here that was normally applied to fugitive slaves. He implies that the Heraklids are subjected to Eurystheus as their father had been, and suggests a stronger claim for their surrender than if they were free citizens.

In historic times many Greek states entered into treaties with each other providing for mutual return of fugitive slaves.

191 *when our sentence was decreed, when we went into exile* Iolaos' own argument is as slippery as Kopreus'. He has already said that Eurystheus decreed the death of the Heraklids (16), and Kopreus has confirmed this (63-64). The Heraklids took flight in order to avoid the death sentence. Now Iolaos says that the Argives exiled them, in order to substantiate his argument that they are no longer under Argive jurisdiction. We suggest that Iolaos is perfectly conscious of what he is doing. He has seen through Kopreus' sophistry about runaways and is giving him a fine contemptuous piece of flim-flam in return.

199 *Trachis* This is a city northwest of Athens, on the coast near Thermopylai. Herakles was here with his wife Deianeira and at least some of his children when he died, as told in Sophocles' *Women of Trachis*. Trachis was accordingly the first place to which Eurystheus sent to hunt down the Heraklids. Keyx, king of Trachis, forced them to leave rather than risk war with Argos.

199 *some small Achaian town* All versions of the legend agree that the Heraklids visited many cities in Greece before they were given refuge in Attika, but except for Trachis none of their names has been preserved. Accordingly we do not know which Achaian town Euripides is referring to here, or whether he may be inventing some anonymous place that gave in to the Argive threats. There were two regions called "Achaia" in Greece, one in the northern Peloponnese, on the shores of the Gulf of Korinth, the other, Achaia Phthiotis, north of Trachis on the southern border of Thessaly. Neither grammar nor geography permits the identification which some editors have made of the "Achaian town" with Trachis itself.

213 *Pelops' son was Pittheus* The dynastic relations traced here and alluded to elsewhere in the play would be generally familiar to the Athenian audience. They are shown in the form of a simplified genealogical table below. The house of Danaos was the ruling house of Argos and Mykenai at the time of the play. The house of Pelops had been established in Elis in the western Peloponnese, and after Eurystheus' death was to spread its power to Mykenai, Argos, and Sparta with the accession of Atreus and Thyestes, both sons of Pelops, and Atreus' children Agamemnon and Menelaos. The house of Erechtheus was the "autochthonous" ruling dynasty of Athens and Attica.

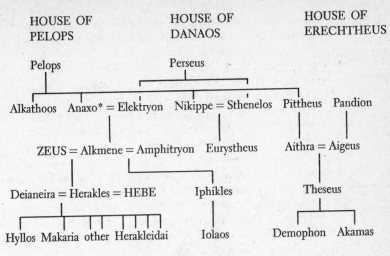

| HOUSE OF PELOPS | HOUSE OF DANAOS | HOUSE OF ERECHTHEUS |

* In some versions her name was Lysidike.

221 *to win the belt of the Amazon queen*   Traditionally this was the ninth labor imposed on Herakles by Eurystheus. The Amazons lived on the northern shores of the Black Sea. Herakles, assisted by Theseus, Iolaos, and others, defeated them in battle, killed their queen Hippolyte and returned her belt to Eurystheus' daughter. Theseus was awarded Hippolyte's sister Antiope as his share of the spoils. By her he was the father of Hippolytos. Demophon and Akamas were his sons by Phaidra. Euripides' *Hippolytos*, which tells the story of Phaidra's disastrous love for Hippolytos, was nearly contemporary with the *Children of Herakles*, being dated in 428 B.C. It is perhaps for this reason that Euripides does not have Iolaos mention to Demophon the specific "debt" incurred by Theseus to Herakles in this adventure—the award of Antiope.

223-24 *Herakles brought your father Theseus/home alive from the blind world below*   Theseus and Peirithoos descended to Tartaros in an attempt to carry off Persephone, Hades' wife and queen of the underworld, as a bride for Peirithoos. They were caught and imprisoned by Hades. In the course of his twelfth labor, the capture of Kerberos (the monster who guarded the underworld), Herakles found them, and released Theseus to return with him.

231-32 *I beg you,/by your knees, your hands, your beard* A suppliant's touching a person's hands, knees, or beard placed that person under a personal obligation to become his protector.

267 *Then banish them. I'll seize them at the frontier* Kopreus is proposing a sordid device by which Demophon can give up the suppliants and avoid religious pollution. Demophon rejects it scornfully. But later when Alkmene proposes a similar legalism with respect to Eurystheus (1054-55), the Chorus do not object.

281 *Touch them, and you'll regret it* The physical threat to the herald should be quite real. In one version of the legend, to which Euripides is alluding, the Athenians killed Kopreus, an act of sacrilege, as he tried to drag the children from the altar. Thereafter, we are told, in certain Athenian processions young men wore black cloaks in ritual commemoration of the murder.

290 *frontiers of Megara* The Greek here refers to Alkathoos, who was king of Megara and a son of Pelops. See the genealogy at the note to 213.

296 *your crops* This refers to warfare as it was practiced in the fifth century, and would be a particularly vivid reminder of the devastation of the Attic countryside by the Spartans at the time of the play's production.

302-10 The meter of this short choral passage indicates excited movement, and the language rapidly becomes colloquial, even comic, as the members of the Chorus speculate on what the herald will tell Eurystheus.

312 We have omitted three lines following this from the translation. Most editors consider them spurious and a later insertion. They may be translated as follows:

> and to marry nobly. A man blinded by passion,
> who marries beneath him, disgusts me. His selfish lust
> leaves only shame to pass on to his children.

The lines have nothing to do with the situation of Demophon (his mother Phaidra was the daughter of Minos, the greatest king of his time), or with Iolaos' intention in this speech.

333-34 *when at last/I stand with Theseus* Iolaos is expecting to meet with Theseus in the underworld after his death. See the Introduction, p. 24.

339-40 *Most men are faint reflections/of their fathers* Iolaos makes explicit here
an important theme of the play: the nobility shown by Demophon
and later by Makaria, Hyllos, and Iolaos himself is unusual and not
to be taken for granted. In the normal course of events, as depicted
by Hesiod in his great parable of the ages of mankind (*Works and
Days*, 109-201), and by many Greek writers after him, the sequence
of the generations of men is a process of decay and corruption. The
characters of the play, until the end, reverse this expectation.

347 *Now I'll go and mobilize the citizens* It is clear that Demophon is speaking
of organizing all Athenians for war, not only the citizens of Marathon or the Tetrapolis. From here on the physical geography of the
play remains Marathonian, but the civic environment is that of
Athens and all Attika. See the note on geography, p. 71.

359-60 *My lord, now we have gods to call on, gods as great/ as any gods of Argos*
In Homeric fashion, Iolaos regards the individual gods here as
champions in battle, fighting for their partisans. At the time of the
play's production, this would be regarded as an old-fashioned and
slightly quaint concept, in keeping with Iolaos' quixotic character.

364-99 This first choral lyric has a strong tight rhythm and popular language suggesting the readiness of the Chorus to participate in military action.
We have assigned alternate passages to the leader and to the Chorus,
speaking antiphonally.

374 *Eurystheus of Argos* The Greek refers to Eurystheus as the son of Sthenelos,
who was in turn the son of Perseus. See the genealogy at the note
to 213.

413 *on high ground, along the ridge* The plain of Marathon is dominated on the
west by the ridge and steep slopes of Mt. Brilessos, also called Mt.
Pentelikos.

432ff. *Now, all over the city* These lines vividly depict a democratic leader trying
to cope with dissent and with criticism of his policies, and create a
highly contemporary background to the play's action.

469 *Surrender me to the Argives in their place* Iolaos' offer to sacrifice himself
appears as the one lapse in his otherwise acute knowledge of himself and the situation. Demophon provides a cool and realistic ap-

praisal of his proposal. But it springs from the same impulses as Iolaos' later effort to join the battle, which is crowned unexpectedly with divine success.

492ff. The Makaria episode: It is not clear whether Euripides invented the story of Makaria or adapted a local tradition. The latter seems somewhat more likely. Pausanias, writing in the second century A.D., relates: "In Marathon there is a spring called Makaria, of which they tell the following tale. . . . An oracle declared to the Athenians that one of the children of Herakles must die a voluntary death, since otherwise they could not be victorious. Then Makaria, daughter of Herakles and Deianeira, slew herself and thereby gave to the Athenians victory and to the spring her name." (I, 32, 6) Makaria's name means "fortunate" or "blessed."

611 *Nothingness is best* Makaria's rationalistic attitude toward death again sets her apart from the conventions of the other characters and specifically from Iolaos, who has given his own view of the underworld at 333ff.

618-19 *I am afraid to speak ill-omened/words of goddess Persephone* Iolaos' deliberate abstention from reproaching the gods is characteristic and contrasts with Alkmene's vocal grudges against Zeus. See 745ff. and 899.

727-35 Again this short choral passage, like 302-10, has been rendered as individual speeches.

769 *and at Herakles' side, I took the city of Sparta!* There is an allusion to the current war with Sparta here. Given the superiority of the Peloponnesian land forces over the Athenian, and the formidable reputation of the Spartan soldier, the idea of "ravaging" Sparta would seem as fanciful to the Athenians of the time as Iolaos' prayer for rejuvenation. Herakles' campaign against Sparta was not connected with his twelve labors, but resulted from a feud with Hippokoon, the usurping king of the city. Herakles killed Hippokoon and many of his sons, and restored Tyndareus, father of Helen and Clytemnestra, to the throne.

774-801 See the Introduction, pp. 20-21, for an analysis of this choral ode.

792 *You are our mother*   The appellation of Athena as "mother" here is extremely unusual. Athena had no mother herself, and was always considered as the virgin goddess. Addressing her as mother of the city would lend a unique urgency to the Chorus' appeal.

796 *honor and sacrifice have always been yours*   These lines refer to the observance of the Great Panathenaia, a festival in honor of Athena held every four years in the month Hekatombaion, corresponding to June/July. The festival culminated on the 28th, or "waning" of the month, with an all-night vigil on the Akropolis, including song and dance by young girls. This was followed the next day by the great sacrificial procession bearing to Athena's temple, the Parthenon, the *peplos* or embroidered robe as a gift for the goddess. This is the procession represented on the Parthenon frieze, now in the British Museum.

841 *and drew the human blood*   The lines can refer only to the sacrifice of Makaria. They appear cursory and cold, but are appropriate in the mouth of the messenger, who had seen many die that day, and was looking to his own advantage from his report.

853 *The trumpets*   The Greek refers to an Etruscan trumpet, which was a long straight military trumpet, supposedly originating with the Etruscans of northern Italy, and copied from them by the Greeks.

874 *Athena's sacred hill at Pallene*   Pallene, on the road from Marathon to Athens, was named after Pallas Athena, and was known in historic times as the site of a shrine of the goddess. Eurystheus was reputedly buried there. See 1063-64 and note.

884 *Hebe* was the goddess of youth, daughter of Zeus and Hera. She was an important figure for Iolaos, not only for this reason, but because after Herakles' death and adoption into heaven, Hebe was given to him in marriage (see 942ff.), sealing his reconciliation with Hera, his old enemy. At this point in the play, Hera abandons Eurystheus.

888 *by the rocks of Skiron*   The rocks of Skiron were in other versions of the story the site of Eurystheus' death at the hands of Iolaos or Hyllos. They were on the seacoast in the territory of Megara, not far from the Isthmus of Korinth and more than sixty miles from Marathon. Euripides' audience would of course be aware of the distance; his intention is to emphasize the superhuman—in fact, Herculean—quality of Iolaos' feat. Skiron had been an outlaw who robbed and

killed travelers by hurling them down the rocks into the sea. Theseus, in the course of a series of heroic exploits not unlike those of Herakles, had overcome Skiron and killed him in the same manner.

901 *I never really believed my son had become a god* Alkmene, Herakles' mother, is the only character in the play who doubts that her son has become a god. Iolaos has stated it as a simple fact at the beginning of the play (12). Her attitude here is of a piece with her character of ignorance and resentment toward the gods.

923-51 See the Introduction, pp. 21-22, for an analysis of this choral ode. We have suggested alternate assignment of lines to Leader and Chorus.

941 *his body consumed in the agony of fire* The Chorus refer to the story of Herakles' death. Consumed by the poisoned shirt of Nessos the centaur, Herakles ordered that he be placed on a funeral pyre on Mt. Oita near Trachis, and that Hyllos, his son, put the torch to it. The Chorus do not deny this part of the legend (the theme of Sophocles' *Women of Trachis*), but rather that Herakles descended to the underworld after his death.

942-43 *With Hebe at his side/ in a bed of shining gold* For the legend of Herakles and Hebe, see the note to 884.

946-47 *They say Athena once appeared/and rescued Herakles* Athena was represented as providing assistance to Herakles from his infancy, when she tricked Hera into feeding the baby Herakles at her breast, thereby ensuring his immortality. She helped him in his struggles with the Lernaian hydra (the second labor) and the Stymphalian birds (the sixth). She fought alongside him against other gods in the sack of Pylos and the duel with Kyknos, and finally received him among the Olympians after his death.

975-77 *You sent a living man down to Hades,/you dispatched him all over the world, made him kill/* Alkmene refers to the twelfth, second, and first labors of Herakles. See the note to 223-24 for the descent to Hades. The Lernaian hydra, a poisonous watersnake, and the Nemean lion were monsters infesting the environs of Argos. Herakles was assigned to kill them.

982-83 *But here in Athens you found/a free city, free men who weren't afraid of you* Alkmene's praise of Athens has a fateful quality. She follows it with the death sentence upon Eurystheus. The city is "free" to choose vengeance as readily as justice and compassion.

988-1010 The distribution of speakers in this passage is hopelessly confused in the manuscripts, but is critical to the meaning of the play. Possible speakers are the servant-messenger, Alkmene, and the leader of the Chorus. Alkmene must be the speaker who is urging Eurystheus' death throughout the passage. Her interlocutor, at least down to 995, must be in our view the servant-messenger. He is the only person to whom Alkmene could address the question: "Hyllos agreed to *that?*" The Chorus have never seen Hyllos. The servant has just come from his master's presence. So far our distribution agrees with that of the Budé editor. It is likely that 998 belongs to the servant; it is quite in character with his earlier plain-spoken attitude. But a new speaker appears to enter the dialogue at 1000, repeating the servant's prohibition against killing Eurystheus from 988. Alkmene too responds as though to a new speaker at 1001. Accordingly we assign 1000 and 1002 to the leader of the Chorus, departing in this from the Budé editor, who assigns both to the servant. This distribution brings the deep division in the Chorus' minds and the transformation of their role somewhat more plainly into view.

1015 *you and I are cousins* In fact they were cousins twice over, their mothers being sisters and their fathers brothers. See the genealogy at the note to 213.

1030 *I couldn't leave one stone unturned* This appears to be the first occurrence of this durable image in Western literature.

1044-45 *I'll take my revenge on you—/the noble vengeance of the dead* Eurystheus here establishes the religious titles by which his body and burial place shall be addressed, and which denote the power inherent in his sepulchre, to be explained in his next speech. The Greek *prostropaion* here means the spirit or divinity to whom a murdered victim turns to avenge his death. Eurystheus will avenge his own murder upon the descendants of Alkmene. *Gennaion,* "noble," refers to his future role in protecting Athens.

1061 *an ancient oracle of Apollo* The Greek term for the god here is *Loxias*, a title used for Apollo, especially in his role as the god of oracles.

1063-64 *Bury my body . . ./before Athena's shrine at Pallene* In other versions of the myth, Eurystheus' head was buried at Trikorythos in the Tetrapolis and his body at Gargettos, a town near Pallene. Euripides' version however undoubtedly reflects a real cult practice in his time, and is consistent with the theme of the play: Eurystheus as protector of Athens is to be associated with Athena's shrine. See the note to 874.

1080 *assure your city's safety* The Budé editor preserves the manuscript reading here, which would give the sense: "my city," or "my descendants." This does not seem possible in the context. Even Alkmene could not twist Eurystheus' prophecy into a promise of safety for Argos or the Heraklids. We accept the more usual emendation.

1084-85 *Kill him!/Throw his body to the dogs* The Budé editor, along with some others, emends the manuscript reading "dogs" (*kysi*) to "funeral pyre" (*pyri*). Alkmene's words are shocking, and the Chorus' agreement with them is revolting. But we do not think that either humane sentiment or consistency is a sufficient reason for altering the reading of the text, especially when it is Alkmene who is speaking.

1085-86 *Dead,/you'll never drive me from my father's land again* Alkmene refers to the oracle which Eurystheus has just produced, prophesying his power after death to influence human events. Alkmene's resentment of the divine utterance and her misinterpretation of it would be in keeping with her character. It might also help to explain her command to throw Eurystheus' body to the dogs. So treated, in her mind he could not live again to plague her.

GLOSSARY

ACHAIA, two regions in Greece, one in the northern Peloponnese, and the other, Achaia Phthiotis, in northern Greece adjacent to Thessaly.

AITHRA, daughter of Pittheus, king of Troizen, and mother of Theseus.

AKAMAS, son of Theseus, co-ruler of Athens with his brother Demophon.

ALKMENE, daughter of Elektryon king of Mykenai; she became by Zeus mother of Herakles.

AMAZON, one of a legendary nation of women warriors, living near the Black Sea. One of Herakles' labors was to capture the belt of the Amazon queen Hippolyte.

APHRODITE, goddess of love and fertility.

APOLLO, god of many of the civilized arts, including poetry, music, healing, prophecy, and the building of cities.

ARES, god of war.

ARGOS, a city and district in the northeastern Peloponnese. At the time of the play's action, it was the principal power in Greece, and was united with Mykenai under the rule of Eurystheus.

ATHENA, daughter of Zeus, the virgin goddess of wisdom, the practical arts and sciences, and war; patron goddess of Athens.

ATHENS, the capital city of Attika.

ATTIKA, the southeastern peninsula of central Greece.

DEMOPHON, son of Theseus, co-ruler of Athens with Akamas his brother.

ETRUSCAN, referring to a region in northern Italy, settled by a people of unknown origin.

EUBOIA, a large narrow island just northeast of the Attic peninsula.

EURYSTHEUS, son of Sthenelos and king of Argos and Mykenai; he imposed on Herakles the labors for which he was famous.

FATES, visualized as three divine sisters spinning, measuring, and cutting the threads of human lives and events.

GRACES, three goddesses signifying beauty or grace.

HADES, god of the dead and ruler of the underworld, which was often named for him.

HEBE, daughter of Zeus and Hera and goddess of youth; wife of Herakles after the end of his life on earth.

HERA, goddess of women and matrimony, wife and sister of Zeus; she was the patron goddess of Argos and the inveterate enemy of Herakles until after his death.

HERAKLEIDAI, the children of Herakles. In this play only two are named, Hyllos and Makaria, but there were younger sons (appearing in the play at the altar), younger daughters (in the temple), and older sons (campaigning with Hyllos). Only a few names are known from other sources: Ktesippos, Glenos, and Hodites. All these appear to be the children of Herakles and Deianeira. Herakles had had children by his first wife Megara, but killed them all in his madness. He also had many bastard children from various liaisons, including Telephos and Tlepolemos, heroes connected with the Trojan war. Tlepolemos is associated in some legends with the later fortunes of the Heraklids of this play.

HERAKLES, son of Zeus and Alkmene; he was among the most famous of Greek heroes, noted not only for the twelve labors he performed for Eurystheus, but for countless other acts of bravery, strength, compassion, and sometimes hot-headedness.

HYDRA, a monstrous and poisonous water-snake with many heads, inhabiting the Lernaian swamp near Argos. It was one of Herakles' labors to kiss the hydra, which he did with the help of Iolaos.

HYLLOS, oldest son of Herakles and Deianeira.

HYMENAIOS, god of the wedding-feast.

IOLAOS, son of Iphikles, who was the son of Amphitryon and Alkmene, and the twin half-brother to Herakles.

KOPREUS, herald of Eurystheus.

MAKARIA, daughter of Herakles and Deianeira.

MARATHON, a town and plain about twenty-three miles northeast of Athens near the sea-coast; scene of the Athenian defeat of the invading Persians in 490 B.C.

MEGARA, a city west of Athens, near the Isthmus of Korinth. It was independent of Athens, and at the time of the play was ruled by Alkathoos, son of Pelops.

MYKENAI, a city of the Peloponnese near Argos; at the time of the play, it was united with Argos under the sovereignty of Eurystheus.

PALLENE, a town in Attika, the site of a shrine of Pallas Athena.

PANDION, son of Kekrops and king of Athens; father of Aigeus and grandfather of Theseus.

PELOPS, son of Tantalos and king of Elis in the western Peloponnese; he was renowned for his wealth. Through dynastic marriages his descendants extended their rule over most of Greece south of the Isthmus of Korinth; hence it was named the Peloponnese, "Pelops' island," after him.

PERSEPHONE, a goddess, Demeter's daughter, Hades' wife, and queen of the underworld, also called Kore.

PITTHEUS, son of Pelops and king of Troizen in the northeastern Peloponnese; father of Aithra, Theseus' mother.

SKIRON, an outlaw slain by Theseus in his youth. Skiron would force his victims to wash his feet, then kick them off his cliff into the sea.

SPARTA, a city in the southern Peloponnese.

STHENELOS, son of Perseus and king of Argos and Mykenai; father of Eurystheus.

THESEUS, son of Aigeus (or of the sea god Poseidon) and of Aithra, daughter of Pittheus. Theseus was a legendary hero, king of Athens, and a friend of Herakles.

TRACHIS, a city in Malis, a region in northern Greece west of Boiotia.

ZEUS, chief god of the Greek pantheon.